WRITE AND PUBLISH A SCIENTIFIC PAPER

A STEP-BY-STEP PUBLICATION GUIDE FOR BEGINNERS

Rafiq Muhammad, MD, MIHMEP, Ph.D.

WRITE AND PUBLISH A SCIENTIFIC PAPER

A Step-By-Step Publication Guide For Beginners

Rafiq Muhammad, MD, MIHMEP, Ph.D.

Rafiq Muhammad, MD, MIHMEP, Ph.D.

Disclaimer:

No segment of this book might be replicated, disseminated, or transferred in any structure or using all means, comprising copying, recording, or mechanical or electronic techniques, or by any data stockpiling and recovery framework without the written consent of the author. While certain segments of this book have benefitted from advanced AI tools, extensive human intervention in the form of editing and revising has been undertaken to ensure its precision, clarity, and reliability.

Notice of Liability:

The information provided in this book is provided without any warranty. The writer will not be liable to any individual or an entity with respect to any misfortunes or liabilities caused by the content and the links provided in this book.

Websites and links

The internet is a fluid medium, and the websites keep changing with time. The links provided in this book are for information purposes only, and the author does not give a warranty for any content, accuracy, or other intended purposes.

ISBN: 978-91-989008-5-9

Imprint: Muhammad Rafiq

TABLE OF CONTENTS

TABLE OF CONTENTS 5

WHO SHOULD READ AND WHAT YOU WILL GAIN 9

WHAT YOU WILL LEARN.. 10

ABOUT THE AUTHOR 12

CHAPTER 1. 13

INTRODUCTION... 13

PRACTICAL PROBLEMS ADDRESSED IN THIS BOOK.. 14

CHAPTER 2. 18

UNDERSTANDING A SCIENTIFIC PAPER 18

IMPORTANCE OF PUBLISHING RESEARCH 18

THE STRUCTURE OF A SCIENTIFIC PAPER... 24

TYPES OF SCIENTIFIC PAPERS... 29

Original Research Articles... 29

Review articles... 29

Case Reports.. 30

Short Communications... 31

Opinion Papers 31

Technical Notes.. 32

Letters to the Editor 32

Data Papers... 33

Methodological Papers 33

Review Letters... 34

Book Reviews... 34

Editorials... 34

Conference Papers... 35

Hypothesis Papers 36
Perspective Papers 36
Protocol Papers 36
Systematic Reviews 37
Meta-Analyses 37
Commentary Articles 38
Interviews 39
Monographs 39
ETHICS IN SCIENTIFIC WRITING 47

CHAPTER 3. .... **49**

PREPARING TO WRITE THE MANUSCRIPT **49**

CHOOSING A RESEARCH TOPIC 50
LITERATURE REVIEW PROCESS 56
FORMULATING RESEARCH QUESTIONS AND HYPOTHESIS 58
CHOOSING THE RIGHT JOURNAL FROM THE OUTSET 62
UNDERSTANDING JOURNAL REQUIREMENTS: 66

CHAPTER 4. .... **71**

WRITING A SCIENTIFIC PAPER **71**

WRITING ABSTRACT 72
CRAFTING THE INTRODUCTION 75
DESCRIBING THE METHODS 79
PRESENTING THE RESULTS 85
DISCUSSING THE FINDINGS 88
WRITING THE CONCLUSION 92
CITING SOURCES AND CREATING REFERENCES 94

CHAPTER 5. .... **97**

REFINING YOUR PAPER **97**

REVISING AND EDITING 98
PEER REVIEW PROCESS 100
PROOFREADING 102

CHAPTER 6. .... **105**

PUBLISHING YOUR PAPER **105**

CHOOSING THE RIGHT JOURNAL 106
JOURNAL SCOPE AND AUDIENCE 109
IMPACT FACTOR AND REPUTATION 110
PEER REVIEW PROCESS AND TIMELINE 112
PUBLICATION FEES 113

CHAPTER 7. ....**115**

SUBMITTING YOUR PAPER TO JOURNAL **115**

SUBMISSION GUIDELINES 115
COVER LETTER ESSENTIALS 116
HANDLING REVISIONS AND REJECTIONS 117
RESPONDING TO EDITORS AND REVIEWERS 119
LEARNING FROM FEEDBACK 122

CHAPTER 8. ....**128**

BEYOND PUBLICATION **128**

CHAPTER 9. ....**133**

ARTIFICIAL INTELLIGENCE ETHICAL USE IN WRITING **133**

OVERVIEW OF AI AND CHATGPT 133
ETHICAL CONSIDERATIONS IN USING CHATGPT 135

CHAPTER 10. ....**140**

PUBLICATION PROCESS CANVAS **140**

STEP-BY-STEP GUIDE TO USING THE EXPANDED PUBLICATION PROCESS CANVAS 144
WHY USE THE CANVAS? 144
HOW THE CANVAS WORKS 145
HOW TO BEGIN WITH THE CANVAS 146

CHAPTER 11. ....**147**

TOOLS AND RESOURCES **147**

LITERATURE REVIEW CHECKLIST (PRISMA CHECKLIST) 148
RESEARCH PUBLICATION CHECKLIST 150
COVER LETTER TEMPLATE 152
RESPONSE TO REVIEWERS TEMPLATE 154
TARGET JOURNAL EVALUATION TEMPLATE FOR SUBMISSION 155
PUBLICATION TIMELINE TEMPLATE 158
SOFTWARE AND ONLINE TOOLS 159
REFERENCE MANAGEMENT TOOLS 160
COMPREHENSIVE TABLE FOR PLAGIARISM CHECKERS 162
COMPREHENSIVE PLAGIARISM CHECKLIST FOR SCIENTIFIC PAPERS 164
ONE LAST THING 166

REFERENCES **167**

Are you just starting your research journey and feeling overwhelmed?

Get my FREE 75-page booklet, **Getting Started with Research Design: A Quick Guide to Qualitative, Quantitative, and Mixed Methods Research**.

Inside this booklet, you will find practical tips, checklists, and clear explanations to help you confidently craft your research question, select the right methodology, plan your data collection, and get them published.

Get the foundation you need to kickstart your research with confidence— click the **LINK to download** your free copy now!

WHO SHOULD READ AND WHAT YOU WILL GAIN

Imagine sitting at your desk, surrounded by stacks of articles, highlighted notes, and a half-empty cup of coffee. Your computer screen glows softly, a blank document open, the cursor blinking expectantly. You take a deep breath, feeling both the excitement and the weight of the challenge ahead—writing your first scientific paper.

"Where do I start?" you murmur, leaning back in your chair. The research you have done, the data you have analyzed, and the questions you have pursued for months swirl in your mind. "How do I present this effectively? What should come first?" You scribble a few ideas on a notepad, then pause. "Is this really the best way to frame my argument?" you wonder, flipping through your previous drafts and feedback notes from your advisor.

Your fingers hover above the keyboard. "How do I craft an introduction that draws readers in? What context do they need to understand my work?" Slowly, words begin to take shape. You think about your audience—other researchers, potential collaborators, journal reviewers. The sentences start to flow, but doubts linger. "Am I explaining this clearly enough? What about the journal's guidelines?" you recall a peer's advice: "Write with clarity— make it easy for anyone unfamiliar with your specific research to understand." You adjust your phrasing, striving to be both precise and engaging.

The journey of writing and publishing a scientific paper is both exciting and daunting. The path to publication is not straightforward. It involves a complex maze of research, writing, revisions, and submissions, often accompanied by moments of self-doubt. Navigating through detailed guidelines, dense formatting rules, and rigorous peer reviews can be challenging, especially for beginners. This book aims to demystify this journey, making the process of writing and publishing accessible and manageable.

This book is based on practical experiences and lessons learned from them. It is here to simplify the writing and publishing journey, transforming it from an overwhelming task into a series of clear, manageable steps. Writing a scientific paper does not have to be intimidating; this book takes you through the entire process—from brainstorming to submission—offering step-by-step guidance designed specifically for graduate students and early-career researchers.

The biggest challenges in writing and publishing scientific papers are often understanding how to organize your manuscript, effectively communicate your findings, meet journal expectations, and respond to reviewer feedback. This book addresses these challenges directly, providing practical tools, clear explanations, and structured guidance to streamline your writing journey.

Whether you are defining your research question, crafting your manuscript, or responding to reviewer comments, this guide provides the support you need to succeed. By breaking down each phase of the process and offering actionable advice, this book will help you transform your research into a well-crafted, impactful paper—one that advances your field and showcases your hard work.

WHAT YOU WILL LEARN

Here is what you will gain from this book:

Step-by-Step Guidance - Clear, actionable instructions for writing and structuring each section of your paper, from the abstract to the conclusion.

Article Types Explained - An overview of different types of academic articles (for example original research, review articles, case reports) to help you select the best format for your research.

Practical Tools - Templates for manuscript preparation, revision plans, and cover letters to help you navigate the publishing process.

Peer Review Insights - Strategies for handling the peer review process, addressing reviewer comments, and managing rejections with confidence.

Valuable Resources - Recommendations for software and online tools to assist with writing, reference management, and staying organized.

Ethical AI Guidance - Advice on using AI tools like ChatGPT and Claude ethically in your writing process, ensuring originality and academic integrity.

This book is not just about getting through the writing and publishing process—it is about making the journey a rewarding part of your growth as a researcher. Let us begin this journey together, transforming your research into a well-crafted scientific paper ready for publication.

ABOUT THE AUTHOR

Rafiq Muhammad, MD, MIHMEP, Ph.D., is a seasoned academic and medical professional with a rich background in research methodology and scientific publishing. He earned his medical degree followed by a Master of International Healthcare Management, Economics and Policy from the prestigious SDA Bocconi School of Management in Italy, and a Ph.D. from the world-renowned Karolinska Institute in Sweden.

With a robust track record in the academic publication of systematic literature reviews, Dr. Rafiq has contributed extensively to peer-reviewed journals, enhancing the body of knowledge in medical research. His expertise extends beyond writing to teaching and mentoring, where he has guided numerous graduate students through the complexities of conducting thorough and effective literature reviews. Dr. Rafiq's multidisciplinary approach ensures his students are well-prepared to excel in both academic research and healthcare management, reflecting the profound impact of his own PhD journey.

In "**Write and Publish a Scientific Paper: A Step-By-Step Publication Guide For Beginners**," Dr. Rafiq distills his years of expertise into practical strategies and insights aimed at helping researchers turn their ideas into well-crafted, publishable papers. Whether you are just beginning your journey or are looking to enhance your writing skills, this book provides the clarity, tools, and support needed to excel in scientific writing and publishing.

This book is based on practical experiences and lessons learned from them. It is here to simplify the writing and publishing journey, transforming it from an overwhelming task into a series of clear, manageable steps. Writing a scientific paper does not have to be intimidating; this book takes you through the entire process—from brainstorming to submission—offering step-by-step guidance designed specifically for graduate students and early-career researchers.

CHAPTER 1.

INTRODUCTION

If you are a graduate student, early-career researcher, or anyone new to the world of scientific writing and publishing, this book is tailored specifically for you. The book breaks down the complex process of writing and publishing scientific papers into simplified, clear, manageable steps, eliminating the confusion often caused by the overwhelming nature of the process. It is designed to simplify the process, making it accessible and manageable, no matter your level of experience.

Whether you are defining your research question, crafting your manuscript, or responding to reviewer comments, this book provides the structured guidance you need to succeed.

Starting the journey of writing and publishing a scientific paper can be both exciting and daunting. When you set out on this path, you are filled with ambition and the drive to contribute to your field. However, as the process unfolds, you might encounter numerous challenges that test your determination. Navigating through detailed guidelines, dense formatting rules, and rigorous peer reviews can be particularly challenging.

The path to publication is not straightforward. It involves a complex maze of research, data collection, writing, and revisions, often accompanied by moments of self-doubt. There may be times when you feel lost, unsure of how to proceed, and overwhelmed by the expectations and workload. It was through these experiences that the need for a simplified, clear, structured guide became apparent—one that could help simplify the process for others.

This book is based on practical experiences and the lessons learned from them. It aims to demystify the writing and publishing process, breaking it down into easy-to-follow steps. Whether you are just starting your research or refining your final draft, this book is here to help.

If you are in the early stages of your research, this book will help you understand what to expect and how to prepare. It will guide you through defining your research question, developing a hypothesis, and planning your study.

If you are already working on your manuscript and finding it hard to navigate the complexities of scientific writing, this book offers practical advice. You will find strategies to overcome challenges, stay motivated, and manage the publication process effectively. It equips you with the tools to visualize, structure, and consider every aspect of your research and publication process in an organized manner.

PRACTICAL PROBLEMS ADDRESSED IN THIS BOOK.

This book tackles complex process of writing and publishing scientific papers head-on (Figure 1.1). By breaking down the process into manageable steps and offering practical tips, this book aims to make the writing and publishing process more approachable and less daunting.

Navigating the Scientific Writing and Publishing Process

Starting the journey of writing and publishing a scientific paper can be particularly challenging for beginners. The detailed guidelines, the pressure of peer reviews, and the need to make a significant impact often leave researchers feeling overwhelmed and uncertain about how to proceed. This book addresses these difficulties by providing a clear, step-by-step approach to help you navigate through dense formatting rules, understand the expectations for each section of the paper, and know how to respond to reviewers.

Developing a Clear Research Question

Formulating a clear and focused research question is crucial yet often challenging for students. This book offers strategies for narrowing down your topic, identifying significant and researchable problems, and developing a strong theoretical framework to guide your study. This foundational step ensures your research is well-structured and impactful.

Conducting a Comprehensive Literature Review

Finding, evaluating, and synthesizing existing research can be daunting and time-consuming. The book provides practical advice on how to efficiently conduct a literature review, including tips on using online databases, organizing sources, and identifying gaps in the literature. This approach ensures your research is grounded in existing knowledge and highlights its contribution to the field.

Selecting the Optimal Article Type

Choosing the appropriate article format is crucial for effectively communicating research findings. This book provides guidance on various article types, consisting of original research, review articles, case studies, and short communications. By understanding the characteristics of each format, researchers can make informed decisions to align their work with the most suitable publication outlet.

Writing and Structuring Your Manuscript

Crafting a well-organized and compelling manuscript is often a significant hurdle for students and early career researchers. The book breaks down each section of a scientific paper, offering detailed instructions and templates for writing the introduction, methods, results, discussion, and conclusion. This structured approach simplifies the writing process and ensures clarity and coherence in your manuscript.

Responding to Reviewer Comments and Handling Revisions

Receiving feedback from reviewers can be both helpful and challenging. This book guides you on how to respond effectively to reviewer comments, prioritize revisions, and resubmit your manuscript. It provides strategies for maintaining a professional tone and addressing critiques constructively, increasing the likelihood of acceptance.

Dealing with Rejections

Rejection is a common part of the publication process but can be discouraging. The book offers practical advice on how to handle rejections positively, learn from feedback, and identify alternative journals for submission. This resilience-building approach helps you stay motivated and persistent.

Leveraging Tools and Resources

Utilizing the right tools and resources can streamline the writing and publishing process. This book recommends useful software and online tools for writing, reference management, and project organization. It also includes templates for manuscript preparation, revision plans, and cover letters, making your workflow more efficient.

Planning for Post-Publication Tasks

Publishing your paper is just the beginning. The book provides guidance on how to promote your research, track its impact, and engage with the academic community post-publication. This proactive approach ensures your research reaches a broader audience and contributes to your field.

Figure 1.1. Practical problems in the process of writing and publishing scientific papers

This book is carefully structured to guide readers through every step of the scientific writing and publishing process.

Chapter 2 provides an essential foundation by exploring the importance of publishing research, understanding the structure and types of scientific papers, and addressing ethics in scientific writing. Building on this, **Chapter 3** focuses on preparation, offering strategies for selecting a research topic, conducting a literature review, formulating research questions, and identifying the right journal early in the process. **Chapter 4** is dedicated to the core writing process, with detailed instructions for crafting each section of a scientific paper, from the abstract to the references. Once the manuscript is complete, **Chapter 5** helps refine it through revising, editing, proofreading, and navigating the peer review process. For those ready to submit, **Chapter 6** and **Chapter 7** provide practical advice on selecting journals, understanding submission guidelines, crafting a compelling cover letter, and effectively responding to reviewer comments and handling rejections.

Moving beyond the publication stage, **Chapter 8** delves into post-publication tasks such as promoting research and engaging with the academic community. The book also addresses contemporary challenges and tools in **Chapter 9**, which discusses the ethical use of artificial intelligence in writing, and **Chapter 11**, which offers a range of templates, checklists, and tools to streamline the entire process. Lastly, **Chapter 10** introduces the Publication Process Canvas, a step-by-step framework to enhance planning and execution, ensuring readers can confidently navigate the journey of scientific writing and publishing.

CHAPTER 2.

UNDERSTANDING A SCIENTIFIC PAPER

Publishing research is more than just a final step in the academic journey; it is a vital part of the scientific process. When you publish your findings, you are contributing to the collective knowledge of your field, offering insights that others can build upon. Your work becomes part of the scholarly conversation, helping to advance understanding and drive innovation. Additionally, publishing is a key to professional growth. It enhances your credibility and reputation as a researcher, opens doors to new opportunities, and can lead to collaborations with other experts. It is not just about adding lines to your CV; it is about making a real impact in your area of study.

IMPORTANCE OF PUBLISHING RESEARCH

Publishing your research is a pivotal step in the academic journey. It not only validates your hard work but also positions your findings within the broader scientific community. The act of publishing carries multiple benefits, each contributing to both personal and collective growth.

Expanding Knowledge - Publishing your findings adds to the collective understanding in your field, allowing others to build on your work.

Career Growth - Having published articles boosts your academic and professional profile, paving the way for career advancements and new collaborations.

Securing Funding - A strong publication record can enhance your chances of obtaining research grants and financial support for future projects.

Navigating the path from completing your research to seeing it published can be complex. Understanding each step involved can help streamline the process and enhance your chances of success. Turning your research into a published work can feel like a marathon, but breaking it down into manageable steps can make the journey smoother.

Here is a roadmap to guide you from start to finish (Figure 2.1):

Idea and Research – Every great paper begins with a spark—an intriguing question or problem that catches your interest. You dive into the research, gather your data, and analyze your results, laying the groundwork for your manuscript.

Writing the Manuscript – With your findings in hand, it is time to write. Start with an engaging introduction that sets the stage for your research. Detail your methods clearly, present your results, and discuss their implications, making sure to tie everything back to your original question.

Choosing a Journal – Picking the right journal is crucial. Look for one that aligns with your topic and has a solid reputation. Consider factors like impact factor, readership, and submission guidelines. The right journal can help your paper reach the right audience.

Submission – Once your manuscript is polished, submit it to your chosen journal. Follow their submission guidelines carefully, which usually include formatting requirements and additional documents like cover letters and conflict of interest statements. Attention to detail can save you from delays.

Peer Review – After submission, your manuscript enters the peer review phase. Experts in your field will evaluate your work for accuracy, relevance, and originality. This step is vital to ensure the quality and credibility of your research. Be prepared for multiple rounds of feedback and revisions.

Revisions – Addressing reviewers' comments is a key part of the process. This can range from minor tweaks to significant rewrites. Respond thoughtfully to each comment and provide detailed explanations of your changes. This stage helps refine your manuscript and improve its quality.

Acceptance – If your revisions meet the reviewers' and editor's expectations, your paper will be accepted for publication. There may be final adjustments and proofs to approve before your work is ready to go public.

Publication – The final step is publication. Your research is now available for the academic community and the wider public to read, cite, and build upon. It is a moment of accomplishment and the beginning of your work's impact in your field.

Understanding these steps can make the publishing process less intimidating and more manageable. Each stage is an opportunity to improve your research and ensure it contributes meaningfully to your academic community. Table 2.1 gives a comprehensive overview of the entire publication process, from initial preparation to post-publication activities.

Figure 2.1. Roadmap to Writing and Publishing a Scientific Paper

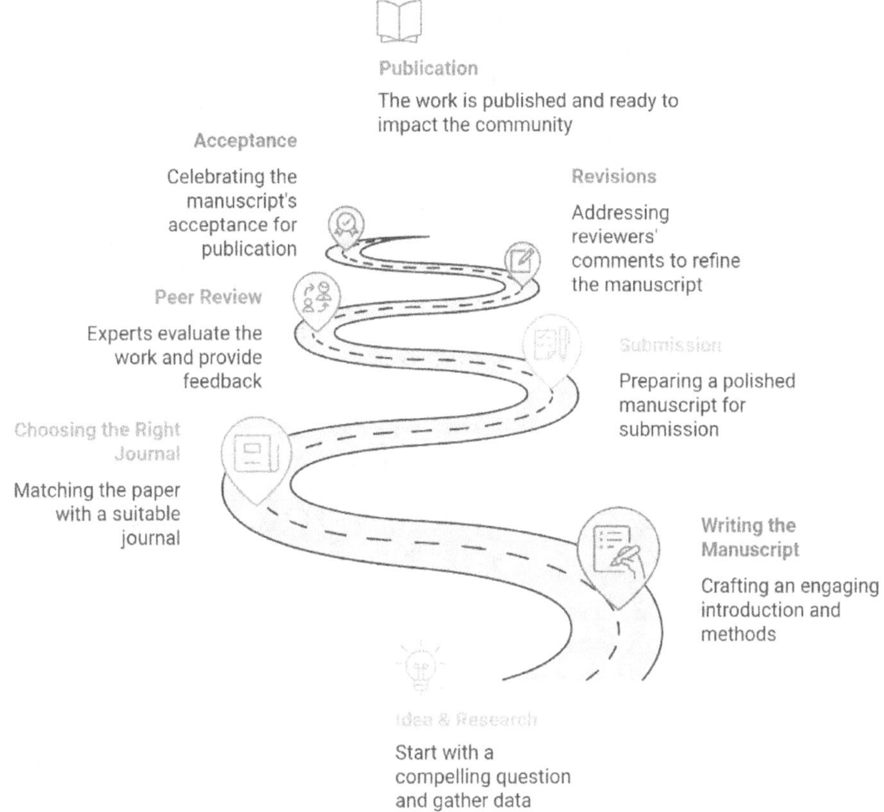

Table 2.1. Overview of the Publication Process

Stage	Task	Description
Pre-Submission Preparation	Literature Review	Perform a comprehensive literature review to ensure your research is unique and contextualized within existing studies.
	Research Ethics	Follow ethical standards throughout your research, including obtaining necessary approvals and participant consent.
	Co-Author Roles	Clearly define each co-author's contributions to ensure transparency and proper acknowledgment.
Manuscript Structure	Abstract	Write a concise, informative abstract that encapsulates your research, methods, results, and conclusions.
	Keywords	Choose relevant keywords to enhance the discoverability of your paper in databases and search engines.
	Figures and Tables	Create clear, well-labeled figures and tables to effectively present your data.
Choosing the Right Journal	Journal Policies	Familiarize yourself with the target journal's policies on open access, publication fees, and copyright.
	Scope of Work	Ensure your research fits within the journal's scope and addresses its readership.
Submission Process	Cover Letter	Craft a compelling cover letter that emphasizes the importance of your work and its relevance to the journal.
	Supplementary Materials	Prepare any additional materials required by the journal, such as raw data, appendices, or multimedia files.
Peer Review Process	Reviewer Selection	Some journals allow you to suggest potential reviewers or exclude certain individuals from reviewing your manuscript.
	Ethical Considerations	Ensure the peer review process is conducted ethically and transparently.
Post-Acceptance	Proofreading and Editing	Conduct final proofreading and editing to eliminate any errors before publication.
	Formatting	Follow the journal's specific formatting guidelines for the final manuscript version.
Post-Publication	Promoting Your Research	Share your published work through academic networks, social media, and conferences to boost its visibility and impact.
	Tracking Citations	Monitor how frequently your work is cited and its influence on your field using tools like Google Scholar and Web of Science.

Handling Rejections	Understanding Feedback	Carefully review feedback from the journal and reviewers to understand why your paper was rejected.
	Revising for Resubmission	Make necessary revisions based on the feedback before submitting to another journal or resubmitting to the same journal if permitted.
Legal and Ethical Issues	Avoiding Plagiarism	Ensure all sources are properly cited and your work is original.
	Data Integrity	Maintain transparency and honesty in reporting and analyzing your data.

THE STRUCTURE OF A SCIENTIFIC PAPER

Crafting a well-structured scientific paper is crucial for conveying research findings effectively. Typically, a scientific paper includes several key sections: Abstract, Introduction, Methods, Results, Discussion, Conclusion, References, and Appendices (if applicable). Each part has a distinct role and enhances the paper's overall clarity and impact.

The following sections offer an overview of the structure of a scientific paper (Table 2.2 & Figure 2.2). A more detailed description of each component can be found in Chapter 4.

Abstract

The Abstract is a brief overview of the entire study, offering a snapshot of the research problem, methodology, key findings, and conclusions. It serves to condense the main aspects of your research into a succinct summary and to entice readers to explore the full paper. The abstract should briefly state the research problem and its importance, summarize the methods used, highlight the key results, and present the main conclusions and implications. To ensure effectiveness, keep the abstract within the word limit specified by the journal, use clear and straightforward language, and include relevant keywords to enhance searchability.

Introduction

The Introduction section of the paper sets the foundation for your research by providing background information, stating the research problem, and outlining the study's objectives. Its purpose is to place the research in context, explain its relevance, clearly define the research question, and establish the specific objectives or hypotheses. This section should summarize existing research related to your topic, identify the gap in the literature that your study addresses, and clearly state the aims of the study. The introduction should engage the reader, follow a logical progression from general background to specific objectives, and clearly define key terms and concepts.

Methods

The Methods section of the paper elaborates how the research was conducted and should provide enough information for others to replicate the study. Its purpose is to describe the research design, procedures, and materials used, ensuring reproducibility. This section should describe the study design, detail the sample size, selection criteria, and demographics, explain the experimental procedures or data collection methods, list the materials, equipment, and tools used, and describe the methods used to analyze the data. Clarity and precision in language are crucial, as is including all relevant details without overwhelming the reader and maintaining consistency in terminology and units.

Results

The Results section is dedicated to presenting the findings of your study in a clear and concise manner. This part of the paper uses a combination of text, tables, and figures to effectively communicate the data and outcomes of your research. The primary goal is to report the study's results accurately, with visuals employed to highlight key data points.

In this section, focus on showcasing the main findings through well-organized tables and figures. Each visual should be accompanied by a textual explanation that describes the data presented. Ensure that results are structured logically, guiding the reader through the findings in a coherent sequence. It is crucial to report the results objectively, leaving any interpretation for the Discussion section.

To enhance clarity, make sure all tables and figures are clearly labeled and referenced within the text. This approach helps readers easily understand and navigate the results of your study.

Discussion

The Discussion section interprets the results, explains their implications, and associates them to existing research. Its purpose is to explain what the results mean in the context of the research question, relate findings to previous research, and explore the broader implications of the results. This section should provide an interpretation of the key findings, compare the results with existing literature, discuss the implications for theory, practice, or future research, acknowledge the limitations of the study, and recommends areas for further research. The discussion should be balanced, acknowledging both strengths and limitations, clear and logically structured, and focused on the most relevant findings and their implications.

Conclusion

The Conclusion summarizes the key results and their implications, focusing on the main takeaways of the study. Its purpose is to provide a brief summary of the main findings and emphasize the significance and implications of the research. The content should include a summary of the key results and findings, discuss the broader implications of the study, and offer recommendations for future research or practice. The conclusion should be brief and to the point, ensuring the main takeaways are clear and focused on the implications and significance of the findings.

References

The References section compiles all the sources cited in the paper and must adhere to the citation style specified by the journal. This section aims to provide thorough citations for every referenced source, thereby bolstering the research's credibility. It should include all essential citation details, such as authors, title, journal, volume, pages, and year, while ensuring consistent formatting in line with the journal's guidelines. Utilizing reference management software can aid in organizing and formatting citations, verifying their accuracy, and ensuring completeness, all in accordance with the required citation style.

Appendices (if any)

Appendices in a paper include supplementary material that supports the main text but is too detailed to include in the main sections. Their purpose is to provide additional information such as raw data, additional analyses, or supplementary material. The content should include materials referenced in the main text but too detailed to include within it. Appendices should be clearly referenced and labeled in the main text, organized logically, and include only relevant supplementary material that adds value to the paper.

Table 2.2. Summary of the Structure of a Scientific Paper

Section	**Purpose**	**Content**	**Tips**
Abstract	Summarize key points and attract readers.	Background, Methods, Results, Conclusion.	Brevity, Clarity, Include relevant keywords.
Introduction	Contextualize the research, state the problem, and set objectives.	Background information, Research gap, Objectives.	Engagement, Logical flow, Clarity.
Methods	Detail procedures to ensure reproducibility.	Study design, Participants, Procedures, Materials and tools, Data analysis.	Clarity, Detail, Consistency.
Results	Present data and findings of the study.	Key results, Tables and figures, Textual description of results.	Clarity, Objectivity, Clear visuals.
Discussion	Explain results, relate to literature, and explore implications.	Interpretation, Literature comparison, Implications, Study limitations, Future research.	Balanced discussion, Clear structure, Relevance.
Conclusion	Summarize findings and highlight their significance.	Summary of key results, Implications, Recommendations for future research or practice.	Conciseness, Clarity, Focus on implications.
References	Cite all sources referenced in the paper to ensure credibility.	Complete citations including authors, title, journal, volume, pages, and year.	Use citation tools, Double-check for accuracy, Follow journal guidelines.
Appendices	Provide additional information that supports the main text.	Supplementary material referenced in the main text but too detailed to include within it.	Clarity, Organization, Relevance.

Figure 2.2. Summary of the Structure of a Scientific Paper

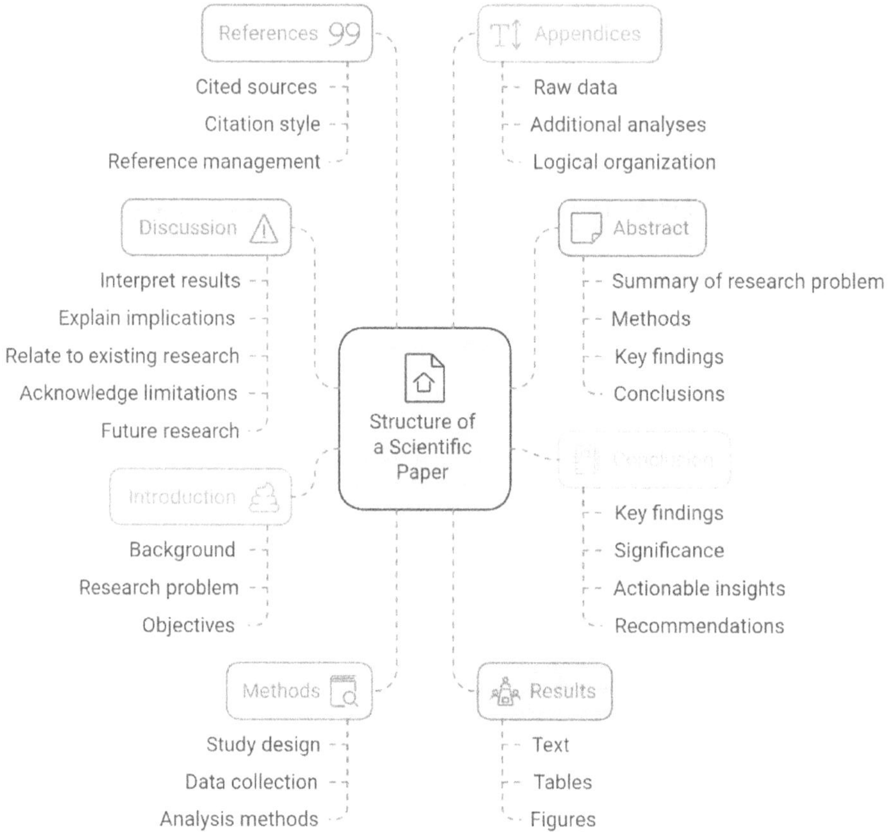

TYPES OF SCIENTIFIC PAPERS

Scientific papers come in various forms, each serving a distinct purpose in the academic and research communities. Understanding the different types of scientific papers can help researchers select the appropriate format for their work and effectively communicate their findings. Here, we explore common types of scientific papers. Table 2.3 provides a comprehensive overview of the types of scientific papers, and Table 2.4 provides a comparison of their types. The following sections outline various types of the scientific papers and details their characteristics.

ORIGINAL RESEARCH ARTICLES

Original Research Articles are comprehensive reports presenting novel research findings. These articles meticulously detail the research methodology, provide in-depth data analysis, and offer insightful interpretations of the results. Typically structured with sections like abstract, introduction, methods, results, discussion, and references, they serve as primary sources of knowledge advancement in their respective fields. Rigorous peer review ensures the articles' quality, accuracy, and contribution to the scientific community.

Key characteristics of Original Research Articles include:

In-depth data analysis - A thorough examination and interpretation of research data.
Detailed methodology - A clear and precise description of research procedures and techniques.
Novel contributions - Presentation of original research findings that expand knowledge.

REVIEW ARTICLES

Review articles provide a comprehensive synthesis of existing research on a specific topic. Unlike original research, which presents new findings, review articles analyze and summarize previous studies to offer an overview of the current state of knowledge. They identify trends, highlight knowledge gaps, and suggest directions for future research. This type of article is crucial for researchers seeking to understand a research area in depth.

Review Articles synthesize and critically analyze existing research on a specific topic, offering an in-depth understanding of the current state of knowledge. Unlike Original Research Articles, which present new findings, Review Articles summarize and evaluate prior studies, highlighting trends, identifying gaps, and suggesting future research directions. They are essential for researchers seeking a comprehensive overview of a field.

Key characteristics of Review Articles:

Comprehensive synthesis - Aggregate findings from multiple studies to provide a broad understanding of the topic.
Critical analysis - Evaluate the strengths, limitations, and implications of prior research.
Identification of gaps and trends - Highlight unaddressed questions and emerging patterns.
Future directions - Propose questions or areas for further investigation.
Types - Include narrative reviews, systematic reviews, meta-analyses, and scoping reviews.

Review Articles guide research by clarifying what is known, what remains uncertain, and where future efforts should focus, making them a cornerstone of scientific progress.

CASE REPORTS

Case Reports provide detailed descriptions of a single or a few clinical cases. These reports often focus on unusual or novel occurrences, such as rare diseases, unique presentations of common conditions, or unexpected treatment outcomes. Case reports can highlight new medical phenomena, contribute to medical education, and inform clinical practice. They typically include sections like Introduction, Case Description, Discussion, and Conclusion.

Key characteristics of Case Reports include:

Unique Cases - Focuses on unusual or novel clinical cases.
Educational Value - Provides insights that can inform clinical practice and medical education.
Detailed Description - Offers thorough documentation of the case, including patient history, diagnosis, treatment, and outcomes.

SHORT COMMUNICATIONS

Short Communications are brief reports that present significant findings or developments in a concise format. These papers are suitable for reporting preliminary results, novel techniques, or important updates that do not require a full-length article. Short communications are typically less than half the length of original research articles and include essential sections such as Abstract, Introduction, Methods, Results, and Discussion. They undergo peer review but are often published more quickly due to their shorter length.

Key characteristics of Short Communications include:

Concise Format - Provides essential information in a brief, focused format.
Timely Updates - Ideal for reporting preliminary results or recent developments.
Rapid Publication - Often published quickly due to their brevity.

OPINION PAPERS

Opinion Papers, also known as perspective or commentary articles, present the author's viewpoint on a particular issue, topic, or recent development in a field. These papers do not present original research data but instead offer insights, interpretations, and recommendations based on existing knowledge. Opinion papers can provoke thought, stimulate discussion, and influence future research and policy. They typically include an introduction to the topic, the author's perspective, supporting arguments, and a conclusion.

Key characteristics of Opinion Papers include:

Author's Viewpoint - Reflects the author's perspective on a specific issue or topic.
Thought-Provoking - Aims to stimulate discussion and debate.
Insightful Analysis - Offers interpretations and recommendations based on existing knowledge.

TECHNICAL NOTES

Technical Notes are succinct reports that describe innovative techniques, methodologies, or procedures within a specific field of study. These articles prioritize practical applications, offering step-by-step guidance, critical evaluations, or enhancements to existing methods. Their focus on utility makes them invaluable for researchers and practitioners looking to adopt or refine tools and techniques in their work.

Typically structured with sections such as an abstract, introduction, methodology, results or application, discussion, and references, Technical Notes aim to deliver clear and actionable insights without extensive theoretical discourse.

Key characteristics of Technical Notes:

Practical focus on new methodologies or tools - Introduce novel techniques or modifications that address specific challenges or improve efficiency and accuracy.
Detailed instructions and evaluations - Provide clear, replicable descriptions of procedures and assess their performance or effectiveness.
Concise and informative presentation - Focus on delivering essential information in a clear, streamlined format, ensuring accessibility to readers.
Emphasis on innovation - Highlight technical advancements or refinements that contribute to progress within the field.
Utility-driven content - Cater to professionals seeking practical solutions, often accompanied by visual aids such as diagrams, workflows, or sample results.

Technical Notes bridge the gap between theory and practice, empowering researchers and practitioners to implement cutting-edge methods and technologies effectively.

LETTERS TO THE EDITOR

Letters to the Editor are short communications that address specific issues or critiques related to previously published articles in a journal. They provide a platform for scholarly debate, allowing authors to respond to criticisms, add additional insights, or discuss the implications of a particular piece of research. These letters are typically brief and focus on a specific point of contention or clarification

Key characteristics of Letters to the Editor include:

Focused Discussion - Addresses specific issues or critiques.
Brief and Concise - Typically short in length, focusing on a single point.
Scholarly Debate - Facilitates dialogue between authors and the research community.

DATA PAPERS

Data Papers are dedicated to describing datasets that have been collected and made publicly available. These articles focus on the methodologies used to collect the data, the structure and format of the dataset, and its potential applications. Data Papers are essential for promoting transparency and reproducibility in research.

Key characteristics of Data Papers include:

Dataset Description - Provides detailed information about the dataset.
Methodological Detail - Explains how the data was collected and processed.
Accessibility - Ensures the dataset is available for use by other researchers.

METHODOLOGICAL PAPERS

Methodological Papers present new methods or significant improvements to existing research methods. These papers focus on the development, validation, and application of new methodologies that can be applied across various studies. They are crucial for advancing research techniques and ensuring the accuracy and efficiency of future studies.

Key characteristics of Methodological Papers include:

Innovative Methods - Introduces new or improved research methods.
Validation - Provides evidence of the method's reliability and validity.
Broad Applicability - Demonstrates how the method can be used in different studies.

REVIEW LETTERS

Review Letters are concise reviews that summarize recent developments in a specific area of research. Unlike full-length review articles, Review Letters provide a quick overview of the latest findings, trends, and significant advancements. These articles are valuable for researchers needing to stay updated on current progress in their field.

Key characteristics of Review Letters include:

Concise Overview - Summarizes recent developments and trends.
Timely Updates - Focuses on the latest research advancements.
Broad Coverage - Provides an overview of a specific research area.

BOOK REVIEWS

Book Reviews critically evaluate new books within a particular field of study. These reviews summarize the book's content, assess its contributions to the field, and provide recommendations for potential readers. Book Reviews help scholars stay informed about new publications and their relevance to ongoing research.

Key characteristics of Book Reviews include:

Critical Evaluation - Assesses the book's content and contributions.
Summary and Analysis - Provides a balanced overview and critique.
Reader Recommendations - Offers guidance on the book's relevance to the field.

EDITORIALS

Editorials are concise articles offering expert insights and commentary on pressing issues, emerging trends, or policies within a specific field. Authored by journal editors or invited specialists, these pieces provide thought-provoking perspectives on the implications of recent research, the state of the discipline, and future directions. Editorials often serve as a platform to stimulate scholarly debate, shape research agendas, and influence the priorities of the academic community.

Editorials are typically written in a persuasive and accessible style, presenting opinions supported by evidence and drawing attention to critical issues requiring attention or action.

Key characteristics of Editorials:

Expert-driven commentary - Written by authorities in the field, editorial pieces provide informed viewpoints grounded in expertise and professional experience.

Focus on current issues and trends - Address timely and relevant topics, such as advancements in research, policy changes, or societal challenges impacting the field.

Influence on research direction - Highlight knowledge gaps, propose innovative approaches, and encourage discourse, often guiding the trajectory of scholarly inquiry.

Concise and opinion-focused - Present arguments clearly and succinctly, often aimed at provoking thought or action among readers.

Editorials play a vital role in fostering intellectual engagement, shaping discourse, and driving progress within academic and professional communities.

CONFERENCE PAPERS

Conference Papers are presented at academic conferences and often published in the conference proceedings. These papers can report on new research, review existing research, or discuss new theories or methodologies. They are a good way to share preliminary findings and get feedback from peers before submitting to a peer-reviewed journal.

Key characteristics of Conference Papers include:

Presentation Format - Prepared for delivery at academic conferences.
Preliminary Findings - Often present early-stage or preliminary research.
Peer Feedback - Provide an opportunity for feedback from the academic community.

HYPOTHESIS PAPERS

Hypothesis Papers propose new hypotheses or theoretical frameworks. These papers are not based on completed experiments but rather on the formulation of new ideas and theoretical insights. They aim to stimulate discussion and future research by presenting a new way of thinking about a problem.

Key characteristics of Hypothesis Papers include:

Theoretical Insight - Propose new hypotheses or theoretical frameworks.
Stimulate Discussion - Encourage debate and further research.
Innovative Thinking - Offer fresh perspectives on existing problems.

PERSPECTIVE PAPERS

Perspective Papers offer an informed opinion or viewpoint on a particular research topic, trend, or policy. Unlike Opinion Papers, Perspective Papers often provide a more balanced view and may discuss both the strengths and weaknesses of different approaches or hypotheses.

Key characteristics of Perspective Papers include:

Informed Opinion - Provide a balanced view on a specific topic.
Critical Evaluation - Discuss strengths and weaknesses of various approaches.
Future Directions - Suggest potential future research or policy directions.

PROTOCOL PAPERS

Protocol Papers describe the planned methods and procedures of a future research project. These papers provide detailed information about the study design, data collection, and analysis plans before the research is conducted. Publishing protocols in advance can enhance transparency and reproducibility.

Key characteristics of Protocol Papers include:

Planned Methods - Describe the methodology of future research.
Transparency - Enhance transparency and reproducibility.

Detailed Description - Provide comprehensive details on study design and procedures.

SYSTEMATIC REVIEWS

Systematic Reviews are a specific type of review article that uses a standardized method to collect, critically appraise, and synthesize research on a particular topic. Unlike traditional review articles, systematic reviews aim to minimize bias by following a rigorous methodology.

Key characteristics of Systematic Reviews:

Rigorous Methodology - Follow a standardized and transparent process, including clear inclusion/exclusion criteria, search strategies, and study selection protocols.

Comprehensive Analysis - Evaluate and synthesize all relevant studies, often employing critical appraisal tools to assess the quality and reliability of the evidence.

Minimize Bias - Reduce bias through predefined criteria, systematic data extraction, and, where applicable, statistical methods like meta-analysis.

Reproducibility - Provide detailed documentation of methods to ensure that others can replicate or verify the review.

Evidence-Based Insights - Offer robust conclusions and recommendations that contribute to informed decision-making in research, policy, and practice.

Systematic Reviews are highly valued for their methodological rigor, enabling them to serve as authoritative resources in advancing knowledge and guiding evidence-based practice.

META-ANALYSES

Meta-Analyses utilize statistical techniques to aggregate and analyze data from several independent studies, offering a quantitative summary of research findings. This study design provides a comprehensive and precise understanding of trends, patterns, and overall effects within a research topic. Frequently conducted as part of systematic reviews, meta-analyses strengthen conclusions by leveraging the power of cumulative evidence, minimizing individual study biases, and increasing statistical reliability.

Structured with sections like abstract, introduction, methods, results, discussion, and references, meta-analyses emphasize transparency in methodology and rigorous data handling to ensure validity and reproducibility.

Key characteristics of Meta-Analyses:

Statistical synthesis of multiple studies - Use advanced statistical methods to combine data, allowing for integration and comparison of findings across studies.

Identification of overall trends and effects - Quantify the magnitude and direction of effects, providing a clearer understanding of relationships or outcomes across a body of research.

Component of systematic reviews - Often embedded within systematic reviews to complement qualitative synthesis with quantitative evidence.

Enhanced statistical power - Increase the reliability of findings by pooling data, especially for studies with small sample sizes.

Reduction of bias and variability - Use systematic methods to address heterogeneity and minimize the influence of outlier studies.

Evidence-based conclusions - Provide robust and generalizable insights, frequently used to inform clinical guidelines, policy decisions, and future research priorities.

Meta-Analyses are a critical tool in evidence-based research, enabling researchers to draw stronger, more reliable conclusions by synthesizing data on a larger scale.

COMMENTARY ARTICLES

Commentary Articles offer a critical or explanatory discussion on a specific issue, often related to a recently published paper. They provide a platform for authors to express their opinions, interpretations, or criticisms of the work, adding depth and perspective to ongoing discussions within the field.

Key characteristics of Commentary Articles include:

Critical Discussion - Provide opinions or interpretations on specific issues.
Relation to Recent Work - Often respond to recently published articles.
Stimulate Debate - Encourage discussion and further investigation.

INTERVIEWS

Interviews present conversations with leading experts, researchers, or practitioners in a particular field. These articles provide insights into the experts' perspectives, experiences, and thoughts on various topics, often offering unique viewpoints not covered in traditional research papers.

Key characteristics of Interviews include:

Expert Insights - Share perspectives from leaders in the field.
Personal Experiences - Highlight individual experiences and viewpoints.
Engaging Format - Present information in a conversational style.

MONOGRAPHS

Monographs are detailed, book-length studies on a specific topic or subject area. These comprehensive works provide in-depth coverage and extensive analysis, often contributing significantly to the field's literature.

Key characteristics of Monographs include:

In-Depth Study - Provide comprehensive analysis and coverage.
Book-Length - Longer format compared to typical journal articles.
Significant Contribution - Offer extensive insights and knowledge on a specific topic.

Table 2.3. Comprehensive Characteristics of Scientific Paper Types

Article Type	Key Characteristics	When to Choose This Article Type	Benefits
Original Research Articles	- Comprehensive data analysis - Detailed methodology - Significant contribution of new insights or findings	When you have new, substantial findings from original research to report.	- Develops skills in conducting and presenting original research. - Contributes new knowledge to the field.
Review Articles	- Summarizes and synthesizes existing research - Critical analysis of strengths and weaknesses - Identifies research gaps and future directions	When you want to offer an overview of current knowledge and identify gaps or trends in a specific research area.	- Enhances understanding of the broader context. - Identifies key trends and gaps in the literature.
Case Reports	- Focuses on unique or novel clinical cases - Provides educational insights - Detailed documentation of patient history, diagnosis, treatment, and outcomes	When you encounter an unusual or novel clinical case that offers valuable insights for medical practice or education.	- Improves clinical observation and reporting skills. - Provides detailed case analysis and insights.
Short Communications	- Concise format - Reports preliminary results or recent developments - Rapid publication	When you have significant findings or updates that can be reported briefly.	- Encourages concise writing and presentation. - Allows for quick dissemination of important findings.
Opinion Papers	- Reflects the author's perspective - Stimulates discussion and debate - Offers insights and recommendations	When you want to share your viewpoint on an issue, trend, or recent development in your field.	- Develops critical thinking and argumentation skills. - Provides a platform for expressing informed opinions.

Technical Notes	- Practical focus on new techniques or methodologies - Step-by-step implementation details - Concise and informative	When you develop a new technique or method and want to provide practical implementation details.	- Offers practical knowledge and hands-on skills. - Demonstrates the application of new methods or technologies.
Letters to the Editor	- Addresses specific issues or critiques - Brief and focused - Facilitates scholarly debate	When you need to address specific issues or provide critiques related to previously published articles.	- Promotes scholarly dialogue and critique. - Enhances skills in succinctly presenting arguments and responses.
Data Papers	- Detailed description of datasets - Methodological detail on data collection - Ensures dataset accessibility and usability	When you have collected a valuable dataset that others in the research community can use.	- Promotes transparency and data sharing. - Enhances skills in data management and documentation.
Methodological Papers	- Introduces new or improved research methods - Provides validation of methods - Demonstrates broad applicability	When you develop or refine research methods that can be widely applied in your field.	- Advances understanding of research methodologies. - Provides a platform for methodological innovation.
Review Letters	- Concise summary of recent developments - Timely updates - Broad coverage of a specific research area	When you want to quickly inform the community about recent advancements in a specific area.	- Keeps students updated on the latest research. - Encourages concise synthesis of current developments.
Editorials	- Provides insights from the editorial team - Discusses current issues or trends - Highlights important topics in the journal	When editors or invited experts want to highlight significant issues or themes for the journal's readers.	- Offers insights into current trends and editorial perspectives. - Encourages critical analysis of contemporary issues.

Book Reviews	- Critically evaluates new books - Summarizes content and contributions - Offers reader recommendations	When you want to inform the community about the relevance and quality of a new book in your field.	- Enhances skills in critical reading and evaluation. - Provides exposure to new literature and perspectives.
Conference Papers	- Prepared for academic conferences - Presents preliminary findings - Opportunity for peer feedback	When presenting your findings at an academic conference and seeking feedback before journal submission.	- Offers opportunities for networking and feedback. - Enhances presentation and public speaking skills.
Hypothesis Papers	- Proposes new hypotheses or theories - Encourages discussion and further research - Innovative thinking	When you have a new hypothesis or theoretical idea that you want to present for discussion and further testing.	- Fosters creativity and innovative thinking. - Provides a platform for proposing new ideas and theories.
Perspective Papers	- Provides a balanced view on a specific topic - Critical evaluation of different approaches - Suggests future research directions	When you want to offer a balanced analysis and suggest future directions for a specific research topic.	- Encourages critical evaluation and balanced analysis. - Highlights potential future research avenues.
Protocol Papers	- Describes planned research methods - Enhances transparency and reproducibility - Detailed study design and procedures	When you want to publish detailed methodologies and plans for future research to ensure transparency.	- Promotes planning and methodological rigor. - Enhances transparency and reproducibility in research.
Systematic Reviews	- Follows standardized review methods - Comprehensive analysis of included studies - Aims to minimize review bias	When conducting a comprehensive review using a rigorous methodology to minimize bias.	- Develops skills in systematic research and review. - Enhances ability to synthesize large volumes of research.
Meta-Analyses	- Combines results from multiple studies - Determines overall trends or effects - Quantitative assessment	When you need to statistically combine findings from multiple studies to identify	- Provides experience in statistical analysis and synthesis. - Enhances understanding of

		overall trends or effects.	trends across multiple studies.
Commentary Articles	- Critical or explanatory discussion - Responds to recent articles - Stimulates scholarly debate	When you want to provide a critical discussion or commentary on recent research articles.	- Promotes critical thinking and scholarly debate. - Encourages engagement with current research topics.
Interviews	- Shares expert insights - Highlights personal experiences and viewpoints - Engaging conversational format	When presenting conversations with leading experts to share their insights and experiences.	- Provides exposure to expert perspectives and experiences. - Enhances skills in conducting and presenting interviews.
Monographs	- Comprehensive in-depth study - Book-length format - Significant contribution to literature	When conducting an in-depth, book-length study that provides extensive insights into a particular topic.	- Offers experience in comprehensive research and writing. - Contributes significantly to the academic literature.

Table 2.4. Comprehensive Comparison of Scientific Paper Types

Article Type	Time Required	Resources Needed	Technical Skills Required
Original Research Articles	High: Requires extensive research, data collection, and analysis	Access to research facilities, datasets, and literature	Advanced research design, statistical analysis, scientific writing
Review Articles	Medium to High: In-depth literature review and synthesis	Extensive access to literature databases and previous research	Literature review, critical analysis, synthesis writing
Case Reports	Medium: Detailed documentation and analysis of individual cases	Access to clinical records, patient consent	Clinical observation, medical writing, ethical considerations
Short Communications	Low to Medium: Shorter format with concise reporting of key findings	Access to preliminary data or recent developments	Concise scientific writing, preliminary data analysis
Opinion Papers	Low to Medium: Based on existing knowledge and perspectives	Nonspecific beyond general access to current literature	Argumentation, critical thinking, persuasive writing
Technical Notes	Medium: Detailed description and evaluation of techniques	Access to new tools, technologies, or methodologies	Technical writing, procedural documentation, practical implementation
Letters to the Editor	Low: Short and focused communication	Nonspecific	Concise writing, critical analysis, scholarly dialogue
Data Papers	Medium: Comprehensive documentation of datasets	Access to the datasets being reported	Data management, documentation, methodological reporting
Methodological Papers	Medium to High: Development and validation of new methods	Access to research tools and validation resources	Method development, validation techniques, methodological writing

Review Letters	Low to Medium: Quick overview and synthesis of recent advancements	Access to recent literature	Literature synthesis, concise writing, current awareness
Editorials	Low: Based on editorial insights and commentary	Nonspecific beyond general access to current issues	Editorial writing, critical thinking, current awareness
Book Reviews	Medium: Thorough reading and evaluation of the book	Access to the book being reviewed	Critical reading, evaluation, concise summarization
Conference Papers	Medium: Preparation for presentation and subsequent paper write-up	Conference registration, travel, and presentation materials	Presentation skills, public speaking, preliminary research reporting
Hypothesis Papers	Low to Medium: Based on theoretical insights and hypothesis formulation	Nonspecific beyond general access to literature	Theoretical writing, hypothesis formulation, critical thinking
Perspective Papers	Medium: Comprehensive evaluation and balanced discussion of a topic	Access to relevant literature and current research	Critical evaluation, balanced analysis, perspective writing
Protocol Papers	Medium: Detailed planning and methodological description	Access to planned research resources and literature	Methodological planning, detailed writing, procedural documentation
Systematic Reviews	High: Extensive literature review and standardized synthesis	Access to extensive literature databases and review tools	Systematic review techniques, comprehensive synthesis, critical analysis
Meta-Analyses	High: Detailed statistical analysis and combination of multiple study results	Access to multiple study datasets and statistical analysis tools	Advanced statistical analysis, synthesis of multiple studies, quantitative assessment

Commentary Articles	Low to Medium: Based on existing research and insights	Access to relevant literature	Critical thinking, persuasive writing, commentary development
Interviews	Medium: Conducting and presenting conversations with leading experts	Access to experts and recording/interview tools	Interview techniques, transcription, narrative presentation
Monographs	High: Comprehensive, in-depth research and writing	Extensive access to literature, datasets, and research tools	In-depth research, comprehensive writing, extensive analysis

ETHICS IN SCIENTIFIC WRITING

Ethics in scientific writing form the bedrock of research integrity and credibility. Upholding ethical standards ensures that research is trustworthy and respected within the scientific community. Key aspects of ethical scientific writing include avoiding plagiarism, proper attribution of authorship and contributions, and managing conflicts of interest. Each of these areas has specific guidelines and best practices to follow.

Plagiarism

Plagiarism entails presenting someone else's work, ideas, or words as one's own without proper acknowledgment. It is a severe ethical breach that compromises the credibility of scientific research and can result in serious consequences, such as paper retraction, reputational damage, and academic penalties. Whether intentional or unintentional, plagiarism is unacceptable in scientific writing.

How To avoid plagiarism?

Proper Citation - Always cite sources accurately using the appropriate citation style as specified by the journal or institution. This includes citing direct quotes, paraphrased ideas, and data.

Original Work - Ensure that your work is original and reflects your analysis and interpretation. Utilize plagiarism detection software to verify the originality of your work before submission.

Quotations and Paraphrasing - When using someone else's words, use quotation marks and provide a citation. For paraphrasing, rewrite the idea in your words and cite the original source.

Reference Management - Use reference management software like EndNote, Mendeley, or Zotero to track all your sources and ensure accurate citation.

Authorship and Contribution

Accurate attribution of authorship is essential for maintaining academic integrity. Each author should have made substantial contributions to the research, from conception to final manuscript. Authorship credit should reflect the specific roles played by individuals, including contributions to research design, data collection, analyses, interpretations, and manuscript preparation. It is crucial to establish clear authorship guidelines and to obtain agreement from all authors regarding their contributions and the order of authorship. For individuals who contributed to the research but do not qualify for authorship, appropriate acknowledgment should be provided.

Conflict of Interest

A conflict of interest occurs when an author's personal, financial, or professional relationships could potentially influence the research process or outcomes. To maintain research integrity and transparency, it is imperative to disclose and manage these conflicts effectively. Disclosing potential conflicts of interest at the time of manuscript submission is essential. Clearly stating these conflicts within the manuscript allows readers to assess the potential impact on the research findings. In cases of significant conflicts, independent review may be necessary to ensure objectivity. Adherence to institutional and journal-specific conflict of interest policies is crucial for maintaining research credibility.

CHAPTER 3.

PREPARING TO WRITE THE MANUSCRIPT

Crafting a research paper requires navigating several essential steps to achieve successful publication. This chapter will guide you through the entire process, beginning with how to select a research topic. We will explore methods for identifying gaps in the literature and choosing a topic that aligns with your interests, ensuring your research is both unique and engaging.

Next, we will dive into how to conduct a comprehensive literature review. You will learn techniques for searching relevant sources, synthesizing the gathered information, and effectively organizing your references. This foundation will help you formulate clear, precise, and testable research questions and hypotheses, which are vital for your study.

Choosing the right journal from the start is another critical step. We will offer tips on selecting the most suitable journal for your work, aiming to reach the appropriate audience and enhance your chances of acceptance. Understanding and interpreting journal requirements will ensure you meet all the necessary criteria for submission.

These preceding steps are crucial in preparing you to write a well-organized and impactful manuscript ready for publication. By following these guidelines, you will be equipped to write a well-organized and impactful research paper ready for publication (Table 3.1).

CHOOSING A RESEARCH TOPIC

The foundation of a successful research project is a well-chosen topic. A strong research topic not only aligns with the researcher's interests but also addresses a significant knowledge gap.

This section outlines strategies for identifying a suitable research focus.

Conduct a Comprehensive Literature Review

Search widely and utilize academic databases such as PubMed, Google Scholar, JSTOR, and PsycINFO to gather a broad range of studies related to your field of interest.

Read extensively and focus on recent publications to understand current trends and advancements. Pay attention to the conclusions and discussions in these papers, where authors often suggest areas needing further research.

Map existing knowledge and create a visual representation (such as a mind map) of the key findings, theories, and methodologies in your area of interest. This helps in visualizing the landscape of existing research.

Analyze Previous Studies

Look for recurring themes and patterns in the literature. This can reveal areas that have been well-studied and those that have not.

Pay attention to the limitations and gaps mentioned by other researchers. These can provide clues about what has not been explored thoroughly.

Look for contradictions and identify conflicting findings or theories. These contradictions can form the basis for new research that seeks to clarify or resolve these discrepancies.

Engage with Researchers and Practitioners

Discuss potential research topics with professors, advisors, and colleagues who are knowledgeable in your field. They can provide insights into gaps in the literature and suggest relevant research questions.

Participate in academic conferences, workshops, and seminars. These events are excellent opportunities to hear about the latest research, identify gaps, and network with experts who can offer valuable feedback.

Examine research proposals and grant applications, if accessible. These documents often highlight perceived gaps and emerging areas of interest in the field.

Aligning Research Interests with Feasibility

Selecting a suitable research topic requires careful consideration of personal interests, expertise, and practical constraints.

Matching Topic with Passion and Expertise

A strong research foundation begins with a topic that genuinely excites and motivates the researcher. Aligning the chosen subject with personal strengths and knowledge can enhance the research process. Furthermore, considering how the research fits into long-term academic or career goals can shape a fulfilling research journey.

Assessing Research Feasibility

To ensure a manageable and productive research endeavor, several factors must be evaluated. The scope of the research topic should be appropriately defined, avoiding overwhelming breadth or excessive narrowness. Assessing the availability of essential resources, including data, funding, and equipment, is crucial. Time management is essential for balancing research commitments with other obligations.

Exploring and Refining Research Ideas

Conducting preliminary research, such as a brief literature review or pilot study, can illuminate potential research avenues. Seeking feedback from advisors and peers provides valuable perspectives and suggestions for improvement. Iterative refinement of the research topic based on these insights ensures its alignment with the researcher's goals and the current state of knowledge (Figure 3.1).

Table 3.1. Step-by-step Preparation for Writing a Manuscript

Element	Description	Check
Conduct a Comprehensive Literature Review		
Search Widely	Utilize academic databases: PubMed, Google Scholar, JSTOR, PsycINFO. Gather a broad range of studies.	[ ]
Read Extensively	Focus on recent publications. Understand current trends and advancements.	[ ]
Map Existing Knowledge	Create a visual representation (mind map) of key findings, theories, and methodologies.	[ ]
Analyze Previous Studies		
Identify Patterns and Themes	Look for recurring themes and patterns. Identify well-studied and under-researched areas.	[ ]
Highlight Limitations	Focus on limitations and gaps mentioned by other researchers.	[ ]
Look for Contradictions	Identify conflicting findings or theories. Use these discrepancies as the basis for new research.	[ ]
Engage with Researchers and Practitioners		
Consult Experts	Discuss potential topics with professors, advisors, and colleagues.	[ ]
Attend Conferences and Seminars	Participate in academic conferences, workshops, and seminars.	[ ]
Review Research Proposals	Examine accessible research proposals and grant applications. Identify emerging areas of interest.	[ ]
Aligning Research Interests with Feasibility		
Matching Topic with Passion and Expertise	Choose a topic that excites and motivates you. Align with your strengths and knowledge.	[ ]
Assessing Research Feasibility	Ensure the topic's scope is appropriately defined. Assess resource availability and manage time effectively.	[ ]
Exploring and Refining Research Ideas		
Conduct Preliminary Research	Perform a brief literature review or pilot study.	[ ]
Seek Feedback	Obtain feedback from advisors and peers.	[ ]
Iterate and Refine	Refine the research topic iteratively based on feedback and insights.	[ ]

Figure 3.1. Iterative Refinement of the Research Idea

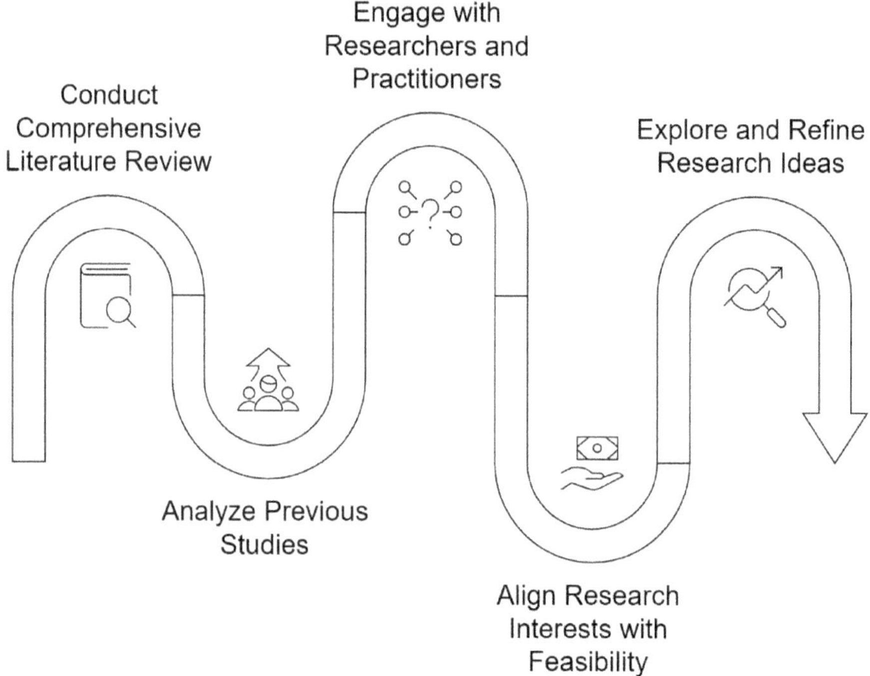

Outcome after identifying gaps in the literature

Once you complete the exercise of identifying gaps, aligning research interests with feasibility, and refining research ideas, you will have a clearly defined, well-justified research topic that:

Addresses a Significant Gap - The chosen topic fills a specific gap in the existing literature, contributing new insights or resolving existing contradictions.

Aligns with Interests and Strengths - The topic aligns with your personal interests, strengths, and long-term academic or career goals, ensuring sustained motivation and engagement throughout the research process.

Is Feasible - The research topic is manageable within the given timeframe and resources. By now, you should have assessed the availability of data, funding, and other necessary resources, and have planned for any potential constraints.

Is Well-Supported - The topic has been refined through feedback from advisors and peers, ensuring it is robust, relevant, and aligned with the current state of knowledge in the field.

Provides a Clear Research Path - You will have a clear roadmap for conducting your research, with defined objectives, a solid theoretical foundation, and a practical plan for data collection and analysis.

Enhances Research Skills - The process of identifying and refining the research topic will also enhance your skills in literature review, critical analysis, and research planning, laying a strong foundation for future research endeavors.

LITERATURE REVIEW PROCESS

A comprehensive literature review is crucial for solid research. By systematically identifying, organizing, and synthesizing existing knowledge, you establish a strong foundation for your investigations.

Locating Pertinent Studies

The first step involves finding relevant scholarly materials. Academic databases like PubMed, Google Scholar, PsycINFO, Web Of Science and JSTOR are primary sources for peer-reviewed articles, books, and conference proceedings. You refine your search results using specific keywords and Boolean operators. University and public libraries provide additional resources, including physical books and journals. Exploring reference lists in relevant studies can uncover valuable sources. Grey literature, such as government reports and dissertations, often offers unique insights.

Managing and Organizing Information

Effectively managing a growing collection of research materials is essential. Reference management software like EndNote, Mendeley, or Zotero helps organize citations, bibliographies, and annotations. Categorizing sources by themes, methodologies, or theoretical frameworks facilitates comparison and analysis. Creating an annotated bibliography that summarizes and evaluates each source enhances understanding of its relevance and contribution. A systematic approach to note-taking, including highlighting key points and using color-coded tags, improves information retrieval. Keeping a detailed search history, including databases used, search terms, and dates, ensures research reproducibility.

Synthesizing Knowledge for a Comprehensive Overview

Integrating diverse research findings into a coherent narrative is key. Identifying recurring themes, patterns, and discrepancies within the literature provides a framework for analysis. Summarizing key findings, methodologies, and theoretical contributions from various sources offers a comprehensive understanding. Comparing and contrasting studies to uncover similarities, differences, and potential explanations deepens the analysis. Critically evaluating source quality, considering factors such as research design and sample size, is crucial for assessing credibility. Finally, drawing conclusions about the current state of knowledge, identifying research gaps, and justifying the need for further investigation completes the literature review process. A well-structured presentation, using headings and subheadings, enhances clarity and readability.

By efficiently searching, organizing, and synthesizing information, you can create a robust literature review that informs your research and situates your work within the broader academic context.

This comprehensive literature review process, involving thorough searching and synthesis, is instrumental in identifying priority gaps within the research field. By highlighting areas that have been underexplored or inconsistently addressed, you can pinpoint the most pressing questions that need further investigation. This systematic approach not only clarifies the landscape of existing knowledge but also guides the formulation of specific, impactful research questions. By identifying these gaps, you can develop well-informed hypotheses that address critical issues, ensuring your studies contribute meaningful advancements to your field. The outcome is a focused research agenda that is grounded in existing literature and ready to fill significant gaps in knowledge, ultimately advancing the discipline.

FORMULATING RESEARCH QUESTIONS AND HYPOTHESIS

Formulating research questions and hypotheses is a fundamental step in the research process, guiding the direction and scope of a study, and providing clear focus and purpose. Well-formulated questions and hypotheses ensure that research is systematic, coherent, and targeted, enhancing the overall quality and relevance of findings. The following sections cover the steps involved in identifying research problems, formulating research questions, and developing hypotheses, offering practical tips, examples, and strategies to create clear, relevant, and testable research questions and hypotheses.

Identifying Research Problems

A research problem is a specific issue, challenge, or gap in knowledge that a study aims to address. Identifying a research problem is crucial as it sets the direction for the entire project, guiding the formulation of research questions and hypotheses. Clearly defined problems keep the research focused and relevant.

Research problems can arise from literature reviews, gaps in existing research, real-world issues, practical needs, and theoretical frameworks. Literature reviews reveal what has already been studied and highlight unresolved questions, leading to significant research contributions. Real-world issues often underscore problems needing immediate solutions, making applied research impactful. Theoretical frameworks provide a foundation for exploring new dimensions or validating existing concepts.

To identify a research problem, techniques such as brainstorming, mind mapping, consulting with peers and mentors, reviewing current trends, and maintaining a research journal are useful. Brainstorming and mind mapping generate ideas and visualize connections. Consulting with experienced researchers provides valuable feedback and suggestions. Keeping abreast of current trends ensures research remains relevant. Documenting observations and ideas in a research journal helps identify potential problems over time.

For example, in education, a research problem might involve factors contributing to the achievement gap in urban schools. In healthcare, it could be the influence of socioeconomic factors on access to mental health services. In technology, it might be barriers to adopting renewable energy technologies in developing countries.

Formulating Research Questions

Good research questions are clear, specific, feasible, and ethically sound, providing precise focus for the study, ensuring manageability and significance. Types of research questions include descriptive, comparative, relational (correlational), and causal questions. Descriptive questions aim to describe characteristics or functions, comparative questions compare groups or variables, relational questions explore relationships between variables, and causal questions determine cause-and-effect relationships (1–3).

Formulating research questions involves identifying the topic of interest, narrowing the focus, and crafting clear, concise questions. Starting with a broad area of interest allows refinement to a specific issue. For instance, a researcher interested in education might narrow their focus to the impact of teacher training on student performance. Crafting straightforward and focused questions maintains clarity and specificity. Table 3.2 presents a checklist for formulating a research question.

Formulating hypothesis

A hypothesis is a prediction that can be tested about the relationship between variables, serving as a foundation for conducting experiments and analyzing data. Effective hypotheses must be testable, falsifiable, clear, specific, and relevant to the research problem. Types of hypotheses include null hypotheses, which assert no effect or relationship between variables, and alternative hypotheses, which assert there is an effect or relationship. Directional hypotheses specify the direction of the relationship, while non-directional hypotheses do not (2,3).

To formulate testable hypotheses, start by reviewing the research problem and questions, identifying the variables, predicting relationships between them, and crafting clear, precise hypotheses. For instance, in education, a hypothesis could be "Students who receive personalized tutoring will perform better on tests than those who do not." In healthcare, it might be "A diet high in fruits and vegetables will reduce the risk of cardiovascular disease in adults." In technology, a hypothesis could be "Improving user interface design will increase user satisfaction with mobile applications."

Table 3.2. Checklist for Formulating a Research Question

Aspect	**Criteria**	**Check**
Understanding the Research Problem	Clearly define the research problem or gap in knowledge.	[ ]
	Identify the significance and relevance of the problem.	[ ]
	Ensure the problem is specific and manageable.	[ ]
Conducting Preliminary Research	Perform a preliminary literature review to understand existing research.	[ ]
	Identify gaps, contradictions, and unresolved questions in the literature.	[ ]
	Note the common themes and key findings from existing studies.	[ ]
Defining the Scope	Narrow down the broad topic to a specific aspect that is feasible to study.	[ ]
	Ensure the scope is neither too broad nor too narrow.	[ ]
	Consider the resources and time available for the research.	[ ]
Aligning with Research Interests	Choose a topic that genuinely interests and motivates you.	[ ]
	Ensure the topic aligns with your expertise and strengths.	[ ]
	Consider how the topic fits into your long-term academic and career goals.	[ ]
Formulating the Research Question	Use clear and concise language to articulate the research question.	[ ]
	Ensure the question is specific, focused, and researchable.	[ ]
	Make sure the question is feasible to answer within the given timeframe and resources.	[ ]
Ensuring Relevance and Significance	Justify the importance and relevance of the research question to the field.	[ ]
	Ensure the question addresses a significant gap or problem in the existing literature.	[ ]
	Consider the potential impact of the research findings.	[ ]
Testing and Refining	Seek feedback from advisors, peers, and experts on the research question.	[ ]
	Conduct a pilot study or preliminary research to test the feasibility of the question.	[ ]
	Refine and revise the question based on feedback and initial findings.	[ ]
Types of Research Questions	Determine the type of research question (descriptive, comparative, relational, or causal).	[ ]

	Ensure the type of question aligns with the research objectives and methodology.	[ ]
	Make sure the question is suitable for the chosen research design.	[ ]
Ethical Considerations	Ensure the research question does not pose any ethical issues.	[ ]
	Make sure the study can be conducted ethically with respect to participants.	[ ]
	Plan for obtaining necessary approvals and informed consent if required.	[ ]
Final Review	Review the research question to ensure clarity, specificity, and relevance.	[ ]
	Verify that the question aligns with the overall research objectives and goals.	[ ]
	Ensure the question is well-structured and easily understandable.	[ ]

CHOOSING THE RIGHT JOURNAL FROM THE OUTSET

Selecting the right journal for your research is crucial for maximizing its acceptability, visibility, and impact. The following sections provide tips to guide you:

Understand Your Research Scope and Audience

Clearly outline the primary field and subfields your research addresses. This helps target journals specializing in these areas.

Determine who will benefit most from your research, such as other researchers, practitioners, policymakers, or a broader audience, and choose a journal that effectively reaches these groups.

Evaluate Journal Relevance and Scope

Thoroughly read the aims and scope of potential journals to ensure alignment with your research focus. This information is typically available on the journal's website.

Examine recent articles published in the journal to see if your research fits in terms of topics, methodologies, and significance.

Assess Journal Quality and Reputation

Consider the journal's impact factor and rankings as one measure of quality and reputation within the field.

Ensure the journal uses a rigorous peer review process to maintain the quality and credibility of published research.

Take into account the reputation of the journal's publisher, as established publishers often offer better visibility and credibility.

Consider Practical Aspects

Decide between publishing in an open-access journal, which can increase visibility and accessibility, or a subscription-based journal, which might have a higher impact factor.

Be mindful of any article processing charges and ensure they fit within your budget. Check if your institution or grants can cover these costs.

Review the journal's submission guidelines for typical review and publication timelines, ensuring they align with your deadlines for graduation, funding, or job applications.

Seek Recommendations and Feedback

Seek recommendations from colleagues, mentors, and advisors who know your work and the publishing landscape in your field.

Use journal ranking lists and databases like the Journal Citation Reports (4) and SCImago Journal Rank (5) to identify suitable journals.

Engage with experts at conferences and through professional networks to gain insights on the best journals for your research.

Match Journal Style and Requirements

Review the journal's submission guidelines to ensure you can comply with their formatting and style requirements.

Verify if the journal publishes the type of article you are writing, such as original research, reviews, case studies, or short communications.

Prepare for Submission

Adapt your manuscript to meet the journal's requirements, including the abstract, keywords, and reference style.

Write a compelling cover letter that explains why your research is a good fit for the journal and how it contributes to the field. Table 3.3 presents a selection criterion for the right target journal.

Table 3.3. Selection Criteria for the Right Target Journal

Checklist for Selecting the Right Journal	Criteria	Check
Understand Your Research Scope and Audience		
Define Your Research Field	Clearly outline the primary field and subfields your research addresses.	[ ]
Identify Your Audience	Determine who will benefit most from your research (researchers, practitioners, policymakers, broader audience) and choose a journal that reaches them.	[ ]
Evaluate Journal Relevance and Scope		
Review Journal Aims and Scope	Read the journal's aims and scope to ensure alignment with your research focus.	[ ]
Check Recent Publications	Examine recent articles to see if your research fits in terms of topics, methodologies, and significance.	[ ]
Assess Journal Quality and Reputation		
Impact Factor and Rankings	Consider the journal's impact factor and rankings as measures of quality and reputation within the field.	[ ]
Peer Review Process	Ensure the journal uses a rigorous peer review process to maintain research quality and credibility.	[ ]
Publisher Reputation	Consider the reputation of the journal's publisher for better visibility and credibility.	[ ]
Consider Practical Aspects		
Open Access vs. Subscription	Decide between an open-access journal (increases visibility and accessibility) and a subscription-based journal (might have a higher impact factor).	[ ]
Publication Fees	Be aware of article processing charges (APCs) and ensure they fit within your budget. Check if your institution or grants can cover these costs.	[ ]
Submission and Publication Timeline	Review submission guidelines for typical review and publication timelines, ensuring they align with your deadlines.	[ ]
Seek Recommendations and Feedback		

Consult Colleagues and Mentors	Seek recommendations from colleagues, mentors, and advisors familiar with your work and the publishing landscape.	[ ]
Review Journal Rankings and Lists	Use journal ranking lists and databases like Journal Citation Reports (JCR) and SCImago Journal Rank (SJR) to identify suitable journals.	[ ]
Network with Experts	Engage with experts at conferences and through professional networks for insights on the best journals for your research.	[ ]
Match Journal Style and Requirements		
Formatting and Style Guidelines	Review submission guidelines to ensure you can comply with formatting and style requirements.	[ ]
Article Types	Verify if the journal publishes the type of article you are writing (e.g., original research, reviews, case studies, short communications).	[ ]
Prepare for Submission		
Tailor Your Manuscript	Adapt your manuscript to meet the journal's requirements, including the abstract, keywords, and reference style.	[ ]
Craft a Cover Letter	Write a compelling cover letter explaining why your research fits the journal and how it contributes to the field.	[ ]

Understanding Journal Requirements:

How to read and interpret author guidelines.

Successfully publishing your research in a reputable journal requires a thorough understanding of the journal's author guidelines. These guidelines provide essential instructions on how to format, structure, and submit your manuscript. Here is a step-by-step approach to effectively read and interpret these guidelines:

1. Locate the Author Guidelines

Visit the journal's official website and navigate to the section dedicated to author guidelines. This is often found under sections labeled "For Authors," "Submit," or "Author Information."

If possible, download or print the guidelines for easy reference throughout the writing and submission process.

2. Understand the Scope and Aims of the Journal

Review the journal's scope and aims to ensure your research aligns with the topics and types of studies they publish. This can prevent rejection due to a mismatch in focus.

Identify the intended audience for the journal to tailor your writing style and content accordingly.

3. Manuscript Preparation

Pay close attention to formatting instructions, including font type and size, margins, line spacing, and page layout. Adhering to these specifics is crucial as many journals have strict formatting standards.

Note the required structure of the manuscript, including sections such as abstract, introduction, methods, results, discussion, conclusions, acknowledgments, and references. Each section might have specific instructions regarding content and length.

Ensure your manuscript adheres to the word count limits for the entire document as well as for individual sections like the abstract or the introduction.

Follow guidelines on language usage, tone, and style. Some journals may require American or British English, or specific scientific terminologies.

4. Reference and Citation Style

Understand the required citation style (e.g., APA, MLA, Chicago, Vancouver) and apply it consistently throughout your manuscript (6,7).

Follow instructions on formatting the reference list, including the order of information (author names, publication year, title, journal name, volume, issue, page numbers).

5. Figures and Tables

Check guidelines on how to format, label, and number figures and tables. Ensure clarity and readability.

Be aware of the acceptable file types (e.g., JPEG, PNG, TIFF) and resolution requirements for figures. Poor quality or incorrect formats can lead to delays or rejections.

6. Supplementary Materials

Some journals allow supplementary materials such as datasets, additional figures, or appendices. Review the guidelines for how to submit these files, including any specific formatting or labeling requirements.

7. Ethical Considerations

Ensure that your research complies with ethical standards and that you have obtained necessary approvals, such as Institutional Review Board (IRB) approval.

Disclose any potential conflicts of interest as required by the journal.

8. Submission Process

Familiarize yourself with the journal's online submission system. Create an account and understand the steps involved in uploading your manuscript and accompanying documents.

Prepare additional required documents such as a cover letter, author agreement forms, and conflict of interest statements.

After submitting, confirm that your submission has been received and is complete. Some journals send an automated confirmation email.

9. Peer Review Process

Understand the journal's peer review process (e.g., single-blind, double-blind, open review) and how it might affect your manuscript preparation.

Be prepared to respond to reviewers' comments and make necessary revisions. Familiarize yourself with the typical timeline for reviews and revisions.

10. Keep Updated

Guidelines can change, so periodically check the journal's website for any updates to their submission requirements or policies.

By meticulously following these steps, you can ensure that your manuscript meets all the journal's requirements, thereby enhancing your chances of successful publication. This attention to detail reflects professionalism and respect for the journal's process, positioning your work more favorably with editors and reviewers.

Table 3.4 presents a checklist to understand the target journal requirements.

Table 3.4. Checklist for Understanding the Target Journal Requirements

Step	Task	Details	Completed
Locate the Author Guidelines	Website Navigation	Visit the journal's official website and navigate to the author guidelines section.	[ ]
	Download or Print	Download or print the guidelines for easy reference.	[ ]
Understand the Scope and Aims of the Journal	Journal's Focus	Review the journal's scope and aims to ensure alignment with your research.	[ ]
	Target Audience	Identify the journal's intended audience to tailor your writing style.	[ ]
Manuscript Preparation	Formatting Requirements	Follow instructions on font type and size, margins, line spacing, and page layout.	[ ]
	Section Structure	Note required sections (abstract, introduction, methods, results, discussion, etc.) and their specific instructions.	[ ]
	Word Count	Ensure your manuscript adheres to the word count limits.	[ ]
	Language and Style	Follow guidelines on language usage, tone, and style.	[ ]
Reference and Citation Style	Citation Format	Apply the required citation style (e.g., APA, MLA, Chicago, Vancouver) consistently.	[ ]
	Reference List	Format the reference list as per guidelines, ensuring correct order of information.	[ ]
Figures and Tables	Formatting and Labeling	Check formatting, labeling, and numbering requirements for figures and tables.	[ ]
	File Types and Quality	Ensure figures are in acceptable file types and meet resolution requirements.	[ ]

Supplementary Materials	Additional Files	Review guidelines for submitting supplementary materials, including formatting and labeling requirements.	[ ]
Ethical Considerations	Ethics Approval	Ensure compliance with ethical standards and obtain necessary approvals (e.g., IRB approval).	[ ]
	Conflict of Interest	Disclose any potential conflicts of interest as required.	[ ]
Submission Process	Online Submission System	Familiarize yourself with the online submission system and create an account.	[ ]
	Required Documents	Prepare additional documents like a cover letter, author agreement forms, and conflict of interest statements.	[ ]
	Submission Confirmation	Confirm submission receipt and completeness; check for an automated confirmation email.	[ ]
Peer Review Process	Review Types	Understand the target journal's peer review process (for example, single-blind, double-blind, open review).	[ ]
	Response to Reviewers	Prepare to respond to reviewers' comments and make necessary revisions.	[ ]
Keep Updated	Regularly Check for Updates	Periodically check the journal's website for updates to submission requirements or policies.	[ ]

CHAPTER 4.

WRITING A SCIENTIFIC PAPER

Crafting a well-organized and coherent research paper requires careful attention to detail.

A standard research paper comprises several key sections. The abstract provides a brief overview, encapsulating the study's purpose, methodology, key findings, and conclusions. The introduction establishes the research context, clearly articulates the research problem, and outlines the study's objectives and hypotheses.

The methodology section offers a detailed account of research procedures, including data collection methods, participants, and analyses techniques. Justifying these choices enhances the study's credibility and reproducibility. The results section presents findings clearly and concisely, often employing visual aids like tables and figures for effective communication. The discussion section interprets the results within the broader research context, comparing them to existing knowledge. It acknowledges study limitations and suggests avenues for future research. The conclusion summarizes key findings, discusses their implications, and offers final remarks.

WRITING ABSTRACT

The abstract is an essential part of a research paper, providing a concise yet thorough summary of the entire study. It allows readers to quickly understand the main points and significance of the research without having to read the full paper.

A well-structured abstract includes several key components that collectively convey the core aspects of the study.

Summarizing the Study

A well-written abstract effectively condenses the entire research study, emphasizing its primary elements. It usually begins with a brief introduction to research topic, followed by a clear statement of the research objective or questions that the study seeks to address. This section should convey the purpose and scope of the research, offering essential context for the reader.

Subsequently, the abstract should briefly outline the methodology used in the study. This encompasses the research design, data collection methods, and analytical techniques employed. The goal is to provide readers with a clear understanding of the research process without excessive detail.

Next, the abstract should present the key findings of the study. This section highlights the most significant results, offering a snapshot of the data and its implications. The findings should be communicated clearly and concisely, emphasizing the main outcomes of the research.

Finally, the abstract concludes with the implications of the findings. This section summarizes the relevance and impact of the research, discussing how the results contribute to the existing body of knowledge and what they mean for future research or practical applications.

Key Elements of an abstract

Introduction to the Research Topic:

- Briefly introduce the subject of the research.
- Provide context and background information to set the stage for the study.

Research Objectives or Questions:

- Clearly state the main objectives or research questions.
- Explain the purpose and scope of the research.

Methodology:

- Describe the research design and approach.
- Outline the data collection methods and analytical techniques used.
- Keep the description concise but informative to ensure comprehension of the research process.

Key Findings:

- Highlight the most important results of the study.
- Present the findings clearly and succinctly.
- Focus on the data that answers the research questions or supports the objectives.

Implications of the Findings:

- Summarize the significance and impact of the results.
- Discuss how the findings contribute to existing knowledge.
- Mention any practical applications or suggestions for future research.

By incorporating these key elements, an abstract provides a condensed version of the research paper, allowing readers to quickly assess the study's purpose, methods, findings, and significance. A well-crafted abstract not only captures the reader's interest but also enhances the overall readability and accessibility of the research paper. Table 4.1 presents a checklist for writing the abstract.

Table 4.1. Abstract Checklist for Research Papers

Element	**Checklist**	**Check**
Summarizing the Study	- Condense the entire study, emphasizing primary elements. - Briefly introduce the research topic. - State research objectives/questions. - Provide purpose and scope of the research. - Outline the methodology used. - Present key findings. - Conclude with implications.	[ ]
Introduction to the Research Topic	- Introduce the research subject. - Provide context and background information.	[ ]
Research Objectives or Questions	- State main objectives or research questions. - Explain purpose and scope.	[ ]
Methodology	- Describe research design and approach. - Outline data collection methods and analytical techniques. - Keep descriptions concise yet informative.	[ ]
Key Findings	- Highlight most important results. - Present findings clearly and succinctly. - Focus on data answering research questions or supporting objectives.	[ ]
Implications of the Findings	- Summarize significance and impact. - Discuss contribution to existing knowledge. - Mention practical applications or future research suggestions.	[ ]

CRAFTING THE INTRODUCTION

A well-crafted introduction is essential for establishing the research context and problem. It provides readers with the necessary background knowledge to appreciate the study's significance. By effectively conveying the research gap, the introduction positions the study as a valuable contribution to the field. To achieve this, it is crucial to present a clear and concise overview of the current state of knowledge, highlighting key studies and identifying areas where further research is needed.

Background Information

The background section of the introduction provides the context for your study. It should offer a comprehensive overview of the current state of knowledge in your research area, summarizing relevant literature and identifying gaps that your study aims to fill. The purpose is to create a foundation for understanding the research problem.

Tips for Writing Background Information

Start Broad, Then Narrow Down - Begin with a broad introduction to the general topic before focusing on specific aspects related to your research. This helps readers who may not be experts in your field to grasp the broader context.

Review Relevant Literature - Summarize key studies, theories, and findings that are pertinent to your research. Highlight what has been done and what remains unexplored.

Identify Gaps and Needs - Clearly articulate the gaps or inconsistencies in the existing literature. This sets the stage for presenting your research problem as a necessary and valuable contribution.

Statement of the problem

The statement of the problem is a critical component of your introduction. It articulates the specific issue or challenge your research aims to address. This section should be concise yet compelling, clearly defining the problem and its significance.

Tips for Writing a Problem Statement

Be Specific and Clear - Avoid vague language. Clearly define the problem in precise terms, making it easy for readers to understand the issue at hand.

Highlight Importance - Explain why the problem is important and worth investigating. Discuss the potential implications of solving or not solving the problem.

Contextualize the Problem - Relate the problem to the background information provided earlier, showing how it fits within the broader context of the field.

Objectives and hypothesis

The objectives and hypothesis section outlines the aims of your study and the predictions you intend to test. This part should be clear and focused, guiding the reader on what to expect from your research.

Tips for Writing Objectives and Hypotheses

Define Clear Objectives - State the primary and, if applicable, secondary objectives of your study. Objectives should be specific, measurable, achievable, relevant, and time-bound (SMART)(8,9).

Formulate Hypotheses - If your research is hypothesis-driven, clearly state your hypotheses. A hypothesis should be a testable prediction that addresses the research problem.

Align with the Problem Statement - Ensure that your objectives and hypotheses are directly related to the problem you have outlined. They should logically follow from the background and problem statement.

Table 4.2 presents a checklist for writing the introduction section of an academic paper.

Table 4.2. Comprehensive Checklist for the Introduction Section

Section	Task	Completed
1. Background Information *Start Broad, Then Narrow Down*		
	Begin with a broad introduction to the general topic.	[ ]
	Gradually narrow down to the specific aspects related to your research.	[ ]
Review Relevant Literature		
	Summarize key studies, theories, and findings pertinent to your research.	[ ]
	Include recent and relevant literature to ensure up-to-date context.	[ ]
Identify Gaps and Needs		
	Clearly articulate the gaps or inconsistencies in existing literature.	[ ]
	Explain the necessity of your research in filling these gaps.	[ ]
2. Statement of the Problem *Be Specific and Clear*		
	Clearly define the research problem in precise terms.	[ ]
	Avoid vague or ambiguous language.	[ ]
Highlight Importance		
	Explain why the problem is significant and worth investigating.	[ ]
	Discuss the potential implications of addressing or not addressing the problem.	[ ]
Contextualize the Problem		
	Relate the problem to the background information provided.	[ ]
	Show how the problem fits within the broader context of the field.	[ ]
3. Objectives and Hypotheses		

Define Clear Objectives		
	State the primary objective(s) of your study.	[ ]
	If applicable, state secondary objectives.	[ ]
	Ensure objectives are Specific, Measurable, Achievable, Relevant, and Time-bound (SMART).	[ ]
Formulate Hypotheses		
	Clearly state your hypotheses if your research is hypothesis-driven.	[ ]
	Ensure hypotheses are testable predictions related to the research problem.	[ ]
Align with the Problem Statement		
	Ensure that objectives and hypotheses directly relate to the problem outlined.	[ ]
	Verify logical progression from the background and problem statement to objectives and hypotheses.	[ ]

DESCRIBING THE METHODS

The methods section is a pivotal part of scientific research, offering a detailed guide to the study's execution. Here, researchers meticulously document the procedures, techniques, and materials used in their investigation. A well-prepared methods section is crucial for ensuring the reproducibility and reliability of the research findings. By clearly outlining the research process, authors enable other scientists to assess the study's validity and potentially replicate it.

Detailed Procedures

The detailed procedures outline every step taken to conduct the research. This section should be thorough enough that another researcher could replicate the study based on your description.

Tips for Writing Detailed Procedures

Organize Logically - Present the procedures in a logical order, typically in the sequence they were performed.

Be Specific - Include specific details such as sample sizes, durations, concentrations, and equipment used.

Use Subheadings - Break down complex procedures into subheadings to improve readability.

Include Illustrations - Where applicable, use diagrams, flowcharts, or tables to illustrate procedures.

Essential components of a thorough methods section include:

Study Design

A clear description of the research design provides the framework for the entire study. It should specify whether the study is experimental, correlational, qualitative, or employs another research design. The design should align with the research questions and hypotheses.

Details to Include

1. **Type of Research Design** - Specify the design type (e.g., experimental, observational, correlational, qualitative, mixed methods).
2. **Justification** - Explain why this design best addresses your research questions and hypotheses.
3. **Variables (NB: Not applicable to all types of studies):**
   - **Independent Variable(s):** What you manipulate or categorize.
   - **Dependent Variable(s):** Outcomes measured.
   - **Control Variables:** Factors held constant to ensure validity.
4. **Population and Sampling** - Define the target population, sampling method, and sample size with justification.
5. **Study Setting** - State the study location (e.g., lab, field) and timeframe (e.g., cross-sectional, longitudinal).
6. **Ethical Considerations** - Address informed consent, confidentiality, and ethics board approval.
7. **Measurement Tools** - Outline tools and techniques (e.g., surveys, experimental setups, coding frameworks).
8. **Limitations and Bias** - Acknowledge potential biases and describe mitigation strategies.

Participants or Subjects

This section describes the study population in detail, including the criteria for inclusion and exclusion. It should also cover the sampling method and any relevant demographic information.

Details to Include:

- Sampling method (for example., random sampling, convenience sampling)
- Number of participants
- Inclusion and exclusion criteria
- Demographic characteristics (for example, age, gender, education level)

Materials and Equipment

Provide a comprehensive list of all materials, instruments, and software used in the research. This section ensures that other researchers can obtain the same materials to replicate the study.

Details to Include:

- Specific names and models of instruments and equipment
- Software used, including version numbers
- Any unique materials required for the study

Procedures

This section offers a step-by-step description of the data collection and experimental processes. It should be detailed enough for another researcher to replicate the study exactly.

Details to Include:

- Sequence of procedures
- Duration of each procedure
- Frequency of data collection
- Specific measurement techniques

Data Analysis

A comprehensive explanation of the statistical or analytical methods used to analyze the data is crucial. This section should also justify the choice of methods and describe any software used.

Details to Include:

- Statistical tests or analytical methods used
- Justification for the choice of methods
- Description of how data were prepared and processed
- Software used for analysis

Ethical Considerations

Addressing ethical considerations ensures that the study complies with relevant guidelines and standards. This section should mention any ethical approvals obtained and how ethical issues were managed.

Details to Include:

- Ethical approval (name of the approving body and approval number)
- Informed consent process
- Measures taken to ensure confidentiality and protect participants
- Adherence to relevant ethical guidelines and standards

Justifying Choices

This section explains why particular methods, materials, and procedures were chosen. Justifying your choices demonstrates the thought process behind your methodology and helps readers understand the rationale for your approach.

Tips for Justifying Choices

Link to Objectives - Explain how each method or choice is relevant to achieving the study's objectives.

Cite Supporting Literature - Refer to previous studies that used similar methods, highlighting their effectiveness.

Address Alternatives - Briefly discuss alternative methods and why they were not chosen, emphasizing the advantages of your selected approach.

Ensuring Reproducibility

Ensuring reproducibility is vital for the scientific integrity of the research. This section should offer enough detail so that other researchers can replicate your study precisely.

Tips for Ensuring Reproducibility

Standardize Procedures - Describe any standardized protocols or guidelines followed during the research.

Specify Conditions - Detail the environmental or experimental conditions, such as temperature, humidity, or time of day.

Include Raw Data - Where feasible, provide access to raw data or supplementary materials to support replication.

Document Equipment - List all equipment and software used, including model numbers and versions.

Table 4.3 presents a checklist for writing the methods section of a academic paper.

Table 4.3. Comprehensive Checklist for the Methods Section

Section	Task	CHECK
Study design		
	Clearly state the type of research design (e.g., experimental, correlational, qualitative)	[ ]
	Justify the choice of research design	[ ]
	Describe the independent, dependent, and control variables (if applicable)	[ ]
Participants or subjects		
	Describe the sampling method used (e.g., random sampling, convenience sampling)	[ ]
	Specify the number of participants or subjects	[ ]
	Define inclusion and exclusion criteria	[ ]
	Provide demographic information (e.g., age, gender, education level)	[ ]
Materials and equipment		
	List all materials and equipment used	[ ]
	Include specific names and models of instruments	[ ]
	Detail any software used, including version numbers	[ ]
Procedures		
	Provide a step-by-step description of the data collection process	[ ]
	Describe the sequence of procedures	[ ]
	Specify the duration of each procedure	[ ]
	Indicate the frequency of data collection	[ ]
	Explain specific measurement techniques	[ ]
Data analysis		
	Describe the statistical or analytical methods used	[ ]
	Justify the choice of statistical or analytical methods	[ ]
	Detail how data were prepared and processed	[ ]
	Specify the software used for data analysis, including version numbers	[ ]
Ethical considerations		
	Confirm adherence to relevant ethical guidelines and standards	[ ]
	Describe the informed consent process	[ ]
	Explain measures taken to ensure confidentiality and protect participants	[ ]

PRESENTING THE RESULTS

The results section of a scientific paper is where you showcase the findings of the research. It should be clear, systematic, and devoid of interpretation or bias. Effective communication of results is essential for understanding the research's implications.

Here are the key elements for presenting your results effectively:

Clear and concise presentation

Presenting your results clearly and concisely is crucial for effective communication. This involves organizing data logically and making the main points easily comprehensible.

The results section should be a straightforward presentation of the data, avoiding unnecessary details or interpretations. The focus should be on reporting the findings accurately and objectively. Using clear and concise language, researchers should describe the outcomes of their analyses without drawing conclusions.

Tips for Clear and Concise Presentation

Logical Structure - Organize the results in a sequence that follows your research questions or hypotheses. This logical flow helps readers understand the study's progression.

Descriptive Headings - Use subheadings to divide the results into sections. Each section should cover a specific aspect of the findings.

Summarize Key Points - Highlight the most important results in the text to ensure they stand out.

Avoid Repetition - Present each piece of data only once. Summarize findings rather than repeating detailed data points.

Use of tables and figures

Tables and figures are essential for showing complex data in a clear and engaging way. They help clarify findings, highlight important patterns, and make the results more visually appealing.

Tables and figures are essential for presenting complex data efficiently. They complement the textual description of the results, allowing readers to quickly grasp key findings. Visual aids should be carefully designed to be informative and easy to understand. Clear labeling, appropriate scales, and concise legends are crucial for effective data presentation.

Tips for Using Tables and Figures

Appropriate Format - Choose whether a table, graph, or chart is the best way to present your data. Use tables for precise numerical data and graphs or charts for trends and relationships.

Clear Labels - Ensure all tables and figures have descriptive titles and legends. Include axis labels, units of measurement, and any necessary notes.

Text References - Refer to tables and figures within the text, explaining their significance. This integration helps readers understand the visuals in the context of your study.

Simplicity - Avoid overcrowding tables and figures with too much information. Focus on the key data points necessary for understanding the results.

Table 4.4 presents a comprehensive checklist for writing the results section of an academic paper.

Table 4.4. Comprehensive Checklist for the Results Section

Section	Task	Check
Clear and Concise Presentation		
	Organize results in a logical sequence that follows research questions or hypotheses	[ ]
	Use descriptive subheadings to divide the results into sections	[ ]
	Highlight key findings in the text	[ ]
	Avoid repetition of data points	[ ]
Use of Tables and Figures		
	Choose the appropriate format (table, graph, chart) for presenting data	[ ]
	Provide clear and descriptive titles for all tables and figures	[ ]
	Include axis labels, units of measurement, and necessary notes in tables and figures	[ ]
	Refer to each table and figure in the text, explaining its significance	[ ]
	Ensure tables and figures are not overcrowded with information	[ ]
	Focus on key data points necessary for understanding results	[ ]
Overall Presentation		
	Ensure the results section is free of interpretation and bias	[ ]
	Summarize statistical findings accurately	[ ]
	Use appropriate statistical terms and symbols	[ ]
	Ensure consistency in data presentation (e.g., units, decimal places)	[ ]
	Include any supplementary materials if necessary	[ ]
Statistical Reporting		
	Report the statistical methods used in analyzing the data	[ ]
	Provide p-values, confidence intervals, and effect sizes as appropriate	[ ]
	Clearly state the significance level used in tests	[ ]
	Include any post-hoc tests or additional analyses performed	[ ]
Data Interpretation		
	Ensure that data interpretation is reserved for the discussion section, and Present findings objectively and factually	[ ]

DISCUSSING THE FINDINGS

The discussion section is where you interpret your research results, relate them to existing literature, and identify the study's limitations along with potential future directions. This section demonstrates the significance of your findings and how they contribute to the broader field of study. Here is how to effectively discuss your findings:

Interpretation of results

Interpreting your results means explaining their significance in relation to your research questions and hypotheses. This section should provide your analysis and insights into the data.

Tips for Interpretation of Results

Relate to Research Questions - Directly connect your findings to the research questions or hypotheses you introduced at the beginning of your paper.

Discuss Significance - Explain the importance of your results and what they mean for the research problem.

Consider Alternatives - Address any other possible explanations for your findings and why you believe your interpretation is the most convincing.

Unexpected Findings - If you encountered any unexpected results, discuss their potential causes and implications.

Comparing with Existing Literature

Comparing your results with existing literature helps to contextualize your findings within the broader field and demonstrates how your study adds to current knowledge.

Tips for Comparing with Existing Literature

Identify Consistencies - Highlight where your findings align with previous research and reinforce existing theories or knowledge.

Discuss Discrepancies - Address any differences or contradictions between your results and past studies, offering possible explanations for these discrepancies.

Integrate Literature - Use the existing literature to support your interpretation and discussion of the results.

Limitations and future directions

Recognizing the limitations of your study and proposing directions for future research are crucial for a balanced discussion and guiding future work.

Tips for Addressing Limitations and Future Directions

Be Transparent - Clearly outline the limitations of your study, such as sample size, methodological issues, or external factors that could have impacted the results.

Discuss Impact - Explain how these limitations influence the interpretation and generalizability of your findings.

Propose Improvements - Suggest ways to overcome these limitations in future research.

Identify New Questions - Point out new research questions or areas that emerged from your study that need further exploration.

Table 4.5 presents a comprehensive checklist for writing the discussion section of an academic paper.

Table 4.5. Comprehensive Checklist for Discussing the Findings

Section	Task	Check
Interpretation of Results		
	Relate findings to research questions or hypotheses introduced in the paper	[ ]
	Explain the significance of the results and their implications for the research problem	[ ]
	Address alternative explanations for the findings and justify your interpretation	[ ]
	Discuss potential causes and implications of any unexpected findings	[ ]
Comparing with Existing Literature		
	Highlight where your findings align with previous research and reinforce existing theories	[ ]
	Address differences or contradictions between your results and past studies, offering explanations	[ ]
	Use existing literature to support your interpretation and discussion of the results	[ ]
	Provide a balanced view by acknowledging both supporting and conflicting literature	[ ]
Limitations and Future Directions		
	Clearly outline the limitations of your study, such as sample size or methodological issues	[ ]
	Explain how these limitations affect the interpretation and generalizability of your findings	[ ]
	Suggest ways to address these limitations in future research	[ ]
	Point out new research questions or areas that emerged from your study that need further exploration	[ ]
	Discuss practical implications of the findings and how they can be applied in the real world	[ ]
General Considerations		
	Maintain a clear and logical structure throughout the discussion	[ ]
	Ensure the discussion is consistent with the results presented	[ ]
	Avoid introducing new results or data not presented in the results section	[ ]

Provide a concise summary of the main findings at the beginning of the discussion	[ ]
Use clear and precise language to avoid ambiguity	[ ]
Emphasize the original contributions and significance of your study	[ ]
End with a strong conclusion that encapsulates the main insights and future directions	[ ]

WRITING THE CONCLUSION

The conclusion of a research paper is where you wrap up your study by summarizing your key findings, discussing their implications, and providing recommendations based on your results. This section should leave the reader with a clear understanding of what was discovered, why it matters, and what steps should be taken next. Here is how to effectively write a conclusion:

Summarizing key findings

The conclusion should start by succinctly summarizing the main outcomes of your study. This section is meant to highlight the most important results without presenting new data or analyses.

Tips for Summarizing Key Findings

Keep it Brief - Condense the key points to provide a clear overview without going into too much detail. This section should remind the reader of the study's essential findings.

Emphasize Key Results - Focus on the most crucial outcomes that directly address your research questions or hypotheses.

Synthesize, Do not Repeat - Instead of repeating the results section, combine and interpret the findings to underscore their significance.

Implications and recommendations

The next part of your conclusion should discuss the broader implications of your findings and provide recommendations based on these results. This section explains why your findings matter and how they can be applied in practice or influence future research.

Tips for Discussing Implications and Recommendations

Discuss Broader Implications - Explain how your findings contribute to the existing body of knowledge and their potential impact on the field.

Provide Practical Recommendations - Based on your findings, offer practical recommendations for practitioners, policymakers, or other researchers.

Suggest Future Research - Identify areas where further research is needed to build on your findings or address any limitations of your study.

Table 4.6 presents a comprehensive checklist for writing the conclusions section of an academic paper.

Table 4.6. Comprehensive Checklist for Writing the Conclusion

Section	Task	Check
Summarizing Key Findings		
	Provide a concise summary of the main findings	[ ]
	Emphasize the most significant results that address your research questions or hypotheses	[ ]
	Synthesize findings to highlight their importance, without repeating the results section	[ ]
Implications and Recommendations		
	Discuss the broader implications of your findings for the field	[ ]
	Provide practical recommendations based on your results	[ ]
	Suggest future research directions to build on your findings or address limitations	[ ]
General Considerations		
	Ensure the conclusion ties back to the introduction and research questions	[ ]
	Maintain a clear and logical structure throughout the conclusion	[ ]
	Use clear and precise language to summarize the study's contributions	[ ]
	End with a strong closing statement that highlights the importance of the research	[ ]
	Avoid introducing new data or analysis	[ ]
	Highlight how the findings contribute to existing knowledge	[ ]
	Ensure the conclusion is aligned with the objectives and hypotheses stated in the introduction	[ ]

CITING SOURCES AND CREATING REFERENCES

Properly citing sources and creating references are crucial aspects of academic writing. Accurate citations and references lend credibility to your work, allow readers to locate the original sources, and help avoid plagiarism. Here is how to effectively cite sources and manage references in your research paper:

Proper Citation Style

Using a consistent and correct citation style is essential for academic integrity and professionalism. Different fields of study often require different citation styles, such as APA, MLA, Chicago, or Harvard (6,7).

Tips for Using Proper Citation Style

Know Your Style - Determine which citation style is required or preferred for your discipline and follow its guidelines meticulously.

In-Text Citations - Provide in-text citations whenever you quote, paraphrase, or reference someone else's work. Ensure these citations include all necessary details as specified by the citation style.

Consistency - Maintain consistency in formatting throughout your paper. This includes punctuation, capitalization, and the order of information in your citations.

Use Citation Tools - Utilize citation management tools like EndNote, Zotero, or Mendeley to help organize and format your citations accurately.

Check Guidelines - Always refer to the latest edition of the citation style manual or guidelines, as rules can change.

Example (APA Style):

In-Text Citation:

"Recent studies indicate a significant increase in crop yield due to improved irrigation methods (Smith, 2018)."

Reference List:

Smith, J. A. (2018). The impact of irrigation on crop yield in arid regions. Journal of Agricultural Science, 56(3), 245-259.

Managing references

Managing references effectively is crucial for maintaining the accuracy and organization of your research paper. Proper reference management ensures that all cited works are correctly listed and easily accessible.

Tips for Managing References

Maintain Detailed Records - Document all sources thoroughly, noting author names, titles, publication dates, and other relevant details.

Use Reference Management Tools - Employ software like EndNote, Zotero, or Mendeley to organize your references, create bibliographies, and format citations as required (10).

Regularly Update Your Reference List - Continuously add new sources to your list to prevent any last-minute rush to find missing information.

Verify All Entries - Ensure all entries in your reference list are complete and correctly formatted. Confirm that every in-text citation corresponds to a reference list entry.

Organize by Source Type - Categorize sources by type (e.g., books, journal articles, websites) to keep the reference list well-organized and easy to navigate.

Follow Submission Guidelines - Adhere to the specific formatting and citation style guidelines provided by your institution, journal, or publisher.

Table 4.7 presents a checklist for citing sources and formatting references in an academic paper.

Table 4.7. Comprehensive Checklist for Citing Sources and Creating References

Section	**Task**	**Check**
Proper Citation Style		
	Determine the required citation style for your discipline	[ ]
	Provide in-text citations for all quotes, paraphrases, and references	[ ]
	Ensure consistency in citation formatting throughout your paper	[ ]
	Utilize citation management tools for accuracy	[ ]
	Refer to the latest edition of the citation style manual or guidelines	[ ]
Managing References		
	Maintain detailed records of all consulted sources	[ ]
	Use reference management software to organize and format citations	[ ]
	Regularly update your reference list with new sources	[ ]
	Verify that all entries are complete and correctly formatted	[ ]
	Cross-check in-text citations with the reference list	[ ]
	Categorize sources based on type (e.g., books, articles, websites)	[ ]
	Follow specific submission guidelines for reference formatting and citation style	[ ]
General Considerations		
	Ensure that all cited works are accurately referenced and accessible	[ ]
	Avoid missing or incorrect citations that could lead to issues of plagiarism	[ ]
	Double-check the spelling of authors' names and accuracy of publication details	[ ]
	Include DOIs, URLs, or other identifiers where applicable	[ ]
	Ensure that the reference list is well-organized and easy to navigate	[ ]

CHAPTER 5.

REFINING YOUR PAPER

Revising and editing your research paper is like polishing a gem—it is where the magic truly happens. This chapter is your roadmap to turning a good draft into a great one. We will kick things off with strategies for effective revision, helping you hone your work with precision and purpose. You will also learn about common pitfalls to avoid, ensuring you do not stumble on the final stretch.

Next, we will delve into the peer review process, a cornerstone of academic publishing. Understanding its importance and learning how to respond thoughtfully to reviewer comments can make or break your publication journey.

Proofreading might seem like a tedious task, but it is the fine-tooth comb that catches pesky errors. I will guide you through thorough grammar and syntax checks, as well as maintaining consistency and clarity throughout your paper.

Finally, we will tackle the art of synthesizing information. Summarizing existing research effectively is crucial for grounding your study in the broader academic landscape. This chapter equips you with the tools to refine, enhance, and perfect your research paper, setting you on the path to publication success.

REVISING AND EDITING

Revision is a vital part of the writing process, requiring significant changes to improve the structure, content, and clarity of your paper. To revise effectively, adopting a systematic approach is crucial.

Strategies for Effective Revision

First, step back from your work by taking a break, which allows you to return with a fresh perspective. Next, evaluate the structure by analyzing the overall organization of your paper, ensuring there is a logical flow and coherence between sections. Then, focus on core ideas by reassessing your main argument, making sure all content supports the thesis. Enhance clarity by refining sentence structure and word choice to improve readability. Finally, incorporate feedback by considering suggestions from peers to identify areas that need improvement.

Common Pitfalls to Avoid

Avoiding common pitfalls during the revision process can save time and improve the quality of your paper.

Common Pitfalls

Forgetting the Thesis - Ensure that every section aligns with and supports your thesis statement. Avoid deviating from the main argument.

Neglecting Flow - Pay attention to transitions between sections and paragraphs. Poor flow can make your paper hard to follow.

Being Wordy - Eliminate unnecessary words and repetitive statements. Strive for conciseness.

Weak Conclusion - Make sure your conclusion effectively summarizes your findings and their implications.

Superficial Revisions - Do not focus solely on spelling and grammar. Deep revision involves enhancing content and structure.

Table 5.1 presents a checklist for revising and editing an academic paper.

Table 5.1. Comprehensive Checklist for Revising and Editing an Academic Paper

Section	Task	Check
Strategies for Effective Revision		
Step Back	Take a break from your work to gain a fresh perspective	[ ]
Evaluate Structure	Ensure your paper has a clear and logical structure	[ ]
	Check that each section transitions smoothly and arguments build coherently	[ ]
	Ensure each paragraph has a clear main idea	[ ]
Focus on Core Ideas	Reassess your main argument	[ ]
	Ensure all sections and paragraphs support your thesis	[ ]
Enhance Clarity	Simplify complex sentences for better comprehension	[ ]
	Improve word choice to avoid jargon and increase clarity	[ ]
	Ensure consistency in terminology and tone throughout the paper	[ ]
Incorporate Feedback	Obtain feedback from peers, mentors, or colleagues	[ ]
	Address constructive criticism and identify areas for improvement	[ ]
	Cross-check feedback with your revision goals	[ ]
Common Pitfalls to Avoid		
Forgetting the Thesis	Ensure every section and paragraph aligns with and supports your thesis statement	[ ]
Neglecting Flow	Improve transitions between sections and paragraphs for better flow	[ ]
	Use transitional phrases to connect ideas smoothly	[ ]
Being Wordy	Remove unnecessary words and repetitive statements	[ ]
	Combine sentences where possible to enhance conciseness	[ ]
Weak Conclusion	Summarize your main findings effectively in the conclusion	[ ]
	Discuss the implications of your findings clearly	[ ]
Superficial Revisions	Focus on content and structural improvements, not just spelling and grammar	[ ]
	Ensure each revision adds value to the overall clarity and coherence of your paper	[ ]

PEER REVIEW PROCESS

The peer review process is a vital step in the journey to publication, where experts scrutinize your research paper to ensure it meets the rigorous standards of academia. Understanding the significance of peer review and learning how to effectively respond to reviewer comments is crucial for getting your work published successfully.

Importance of Peer Review

Peer review plays several essential roles in the academic and research community:

Maintaining Quality - Peer review helps uphold the integrity of research by ensuring that only thoroughly vetted and well-conducted studies are published. Reviewers examine the methodology, accuracy of results, and validity of conclusions.

Offering Constructive Feedback - Reviewers provide valuable feedback to enhance the clarity, coherence, and impact of your paper. They might suggest additional experiments, offer alternative interpretations, or point out areas needing further explanation.

Building Credibility - Having your work peer-reviewed and published in respected journals boosts your credibility as a researcher. It indicates that your research has been evaluated and validated by experts in your field.

Advancing Knowledge - Peer review ensures that only reliable and valuable research contributes to the academic field, preventing the spread of flawed or unsupported findings.

Responding to Reviewer Comments

Handling reviewer feedback well is a key part of the peer review process. Thoughtful and detailed responses can greatly improve the chances of your paper being accepted.

Tips for Responding to Reviewer Comments

Be Respectful and Professional - Always reply to reviewer comments with respect and professionalism, even when you disagree. Reviewers are experts who have volunteered their time to help improve your work.

Understand the Feedback - Read each comment carefully and make sure you fully understand it before responding. Differentiate between major issues that need significant changes and minor points that are easier to address.

Organize Your Responses - Create a response document where you list each reviewer comment followed by your response and any changes you made to the manuscript. Numbering the comments can help keep things organized.

Be Thorough - Provide detailed answers to each comment. Explain how you addressed the issue, or if you disagree, give a clear and reasoned explanation.

Highlight Changes - Clearly show where you made changes in the manuscript. Use different text colors or highlighting to indicate revisions.

Stay Positive - Keep a positive tone in your responses. Acknowledge the value of the feedback and express gratitude for the reviewers' efforts.

PROOFREADING

Proofreading is the last step in the writing process, dedicated to spotting and fixing errors in grammar, syntax, consistency, and clarity (Table 5.2). This important stage ensures that your research paper is polished, professional, and free of mistakes that could affect your credibility. Here is how to approach proofreading effectively:

Grammar and Syntax Checks

Ensuring correct grammar and syntax is vital for producing clear and professional writing. Mistakes in these areas can cause confusion and reduce the quality of your paper.

Tips for Checking Grammar and Syntax

Utilize Grammar Tools – Tools like Grammarly and Microsoft Word's grammar checker can help identify common errors. However, do not rely exclusively on these tools, as they may miss context-specific mistakes.

Read Aloud - Reading your paper aloud can help you detect errors that are easily overlooked when reading silently. This method also helps to spot awkward or overly complex sentences.

Verify Subject Verb Agreement - Make sure that subjects and verbs agree in both number and tense. For example, "The data shows" should be "The data show" because "data" is a plural noun.

Examine Punctuation - Proper punctuation is crucial for readability. Check for missing commas, misplaced apostrophes, and ensure the correct use of periods, colons, and semicolons.

Watch for Common Errors - Be vigilant for commonly confused words (e.g., their/there/they are, affect/effect) and ensure they are used correctly.

Consistency and Clarity

Consistency and clarity are key to ensuring that your paper is easily understood and free of contradictions. Inconsistencies can confuse readers and reduce the impact of your work.

Tips for Ensuring Consistency and Clarity

Maintain Consistent Terminology - Use the same terms throughout your paper. For instance, do not switch between "participants" and "subjects" unless there is a clear reason for the distinction.

Consistent Formatting - Ensure that headings, subheadings, fonts, and citation styles are uniform throughout the paper. This includes consistent use of abbreviations and acronyms.

Clear and Concise Language - Avoid jargon and overly complex sentences. Aim for simplicity and clarity to make your paper accessible to a broader audience.

Check for Logical Flow - Ensure that your arguments progress logically from one point to the next. Each paragraph should build on the previous one, leading to a coherent and persuasive narrative.

Eliminate Redundancy - Remove repetitive statements or redundant information that does not add value to your paper.

Table 5.2. Comprehensive Proofreading Checklist for Academic Papers

Task	**Check**
Run your paper through grammar checkers like Grammarly or Microsoft Word to catch common mistakes. However, double-check manually for context-specific errors.	[ ]
Read your paper out loud to catch mistakes that are easy to miss when reading silently. This can also help identify awkward or overly complex sentences.	[ ]
Verify that subjects and verbs agree in number and tense. For example, "The data shows" should be "The data show" since "data" is plural.	[ ]
Ensure proper use of punctuation marks. Check for missing commas, misplaced apostrophes, and correct usage of periods, colons, and semicolons.	[ ]
*Look for commonly confused words (e.g., their/there/**they are**, affect/effect) and ensure they are used correctly.*	[ ]
*Use the same terms consistently throughout your paper. For example, **do not** alternate between "participants" and "subjects" unless necessary.*	[ ]
Check that headings, subheadings, fonts, and citation styles are consistent throughout the paper. Also, ensure uniform use of abbreviations and acronyms.	[ ]
Avoid jargon and overly complex sentences. Aim for simplicity and clarity to make your paper accessible to a broader audience.	[ ]
Ensure that your arguments progress logically. Each paragraph should build on the previous one, leading to a coherent and persuasive narrative.	[ ]
Remove repetitive statements or redundant information that do not add value to your paper.	[ ]
Step away from your paper for a few hours or even a day. Returning with fresh eyes can help you spot errors more effectively.	[ ]
Proofreading on paper can help you notice mistakes you might miss on a screen. Print out your paper and mark errors with a pen.	[ ]
Ensure all citations are accurate and complete. Verify that every in-text citation matches an entry in the reference list and follows the required citation style.	[ ]
Have a peer or mentor review your paper. A fresh perspective can catch errors and suggest improvements you might have overlooked.	[ ]
Make a personalized proofreading checklist based on common errors you tend to make. Use this list to systematically check your paper.	[ ]

CHAPTER 6.

PUBLISHING YOUR PAPER

Choosing the right journal for your research is a pivotal step on the road to publication. The journal you select will influence how your work is received, who engages with it, and how it impacts the broader academic community. In this chapter, we will discuss the essential factors to consider when selecting a journal, beginning with an understanding of the journal's scope and target audience. It is crucial to find a journal that not only fits your research topic but also reaches the intended readership.

We will also explore the importance of impact factor and reputation. Although these metrics should not be the only criteria, they do influence how your work is viewed within your field. Additionally, we will walk you through the peer review process, outlining what to expect in terms of timelines and feedback, so you can be well-prepared.

Lastly, we will address the often-overlooked issue of publication costs. Being aware of potential expenses can help you plan and avoid unexpected financial surprises. By the end of this chapter, you will be equipped with the knowledge to navigate the journal selection process confidently, ensuring that your research reaches the most appropriate audience.

CHOOSING THE RIGHT JOURNAL

Selecting the appropriate journal is crucial for maximizing the visibility and impact of research findings. Careful consideration of several key factors is essential in this process.

Aligning Research with Journal Scope and Audience

Understanding a journal's focus and target audience is fundamental. The journal's aims and scope should align closely with the research topic. Researchers must consider who will benefit most from their findings to select a journal that effectively reaches the target audience. For instance, research on renewable energy would be better suited for journals specializing in environmental science or sustainable technology than general science publications.

Assessing Journal Quality and Impact

Evaluating a journal's impact factor, reputation, and indexing status is crucial. While impact factor provides a measure of influence, it should be considered alongside other factors. A journal's reputation within the field and its inclusion in major databases like PubMed, Web of Science, or Scopus enhance its visibility and accessibility.

Adhering to Journal Guidelines and Ethics

Thorough review of a journal's submission guidelines is essential. Adherence to formatting, structure, and article type requirements is crucial. Understanding the journal's review process, including the type of peer review and publication timeline, helps manage expectations. Prioritizing journals with high ethical standards, such as those affiliated with the Committee on Publication Ethics (COPE), ensures the integrity of the research.

Leveraging Tools and Seeking Guidance

Online tools like Elsevier's Journal Finder, Springer's Journal Suggester, or Wiley's Journal Finder can assist in identifying potential journals based on manuscript details. Seeking advice from colleagues, mentors, or advisors with publishing experience can provide valuable insights.

By carefully considering these factors, researchers can increase the likelihood of their work being published in a journal that maximizes its impact and visibility within the academic community. Table 6.1 presents a step-by-step approach to selecting the target journal for your article.

Table 6.1. Step-by-Step Guide for Journal Selection

Step	**Action Item**	**Details**
1. Define Your Objectives	**Identify Your Goals**	Determine what you want to achieve with your publication (e.g., reaching a specific audience, maximizing citations).
	Assess Your Research	Consider the type, scope, and significance of your research to narrow down potential journals.
2. Understand Journal Scope and Audience	**Review Journal Scopes**	Look at the aims and scope sections of potential journals to ensure they align with your research topic and content.
	Identify Target Audience	Choose journals whose readership would benefit most from your research findings.
3. Assess Journal Quality and Impact	**Check Impact Factor**	Examine the impact factor, which measures the average number of citations to recent articles. Higher impact factors usually indicate more influential journals.
	Consider Reputation	Evaluate the journal's standing within your field.
	Verify Indexing	Ensure the journal is indexed in major databases like PubMed, Web of Science, or Scopus.
4. Review Submission Guidelines and Requirements	**Read Guidelines**	Review the journal's submission guidelines for specific formatting, structure, and length requirements.
	Check Article Types	Verify if the journal accepts the type of article you are submitting (e.g., original research, review articles).
	Consider Open Access	Decide if you want your paper to be open access. Open access can increase the reach and impact of your work.

5. Evaluate the Review Process	**Understand Peer Review**	Investigate the journal's review process. Double-blind peer review ensures impartiality and fairness.
	Check Review Time	Look at the average time from submission to publication.
6. Consider Journal Ethics and Policies	**Check Ethical Standards**	Ensure the journal adheres to high ethical standards, including guidelines on plagiarism, data fabrication.
	Review Author Rights	Examine the journal's policies on author rights and copyright.
7. Utilize Journal Selection Tools	**Use Online Tools**	Leverage tools like Elsevier's Journal Finder, Springer's Journal Suggester, or Wiley's Journal Finder.
	Seek Recommendations	Consult colleagues, mentors, and advisors who have experience in publishing.
8. Final Decision and Submission	**Compare Options**	Weigh the pros and cons of your shortlisted journals based on the criteria outlined above.
	Submit Your Manuscript	Prepare your manuscript according to the journal's guidelines and submit it.

JOURNAL SCOPE AND AUDIENCE

Selecting the optimal journal for research dissemination is crucial. This involves carefully considering a journal's scope, target audience, and other relevant factors.

Understanding Journal Scope and Audience

A journal's "Aims and Scope" section outlines its focus, accepted topics, and target audience. Aligning research with these parameters increases the likelihood of acceptance. Researchers must identify who will benefit most from their findings to select a journal that reaches the appropriate audience. For example, research on renewable energy aligns well with journals specializing in environmental science or sustainable technology. Interdisciplinary research may benefit from journals that welcome a broader scope of inquiry.

Assessing Journal Quality and Impact

Beyond alignment, journal quality and impact matter. Factors such as impact factor, reputation, and indexing in major databases influence a journal's visibility. A journal with a strong reputation and a rigorous peer review process is generally preferred. Additionally, consider the journal's readership and whether it includes key figures in the field.

Maximizing Research Reach and Impact

A journal's engagement with its audience, including social media presence and open access options, can influence research impact. Open access journals often have broader readership, while some journals have a stronger regional focus. Aligning the journal's reach with the research's target audience is essential for maximizing its impact.

IMPACT FACTOR AND REPUTATION

When selecting a journal for your research paper, the impact factor and the reputation of the journal play significant roles. These metrics help you assess the journal's influence and credibility within the academic community. The impact factor is a measure that highlights the yearly average number of citations to recent articles published in a particular journal. It is used to gauge the significance or rank of a journal by calculating the frequency with which the average article in a journal has been cited in a particular year. A high impact factor indicates that the journal's articles are frequently cited by other researchers, suggesting that the journal has a strong influence in its field.

For instance, journals like "Nature" and "The New England Journal of Medicine" have high impact factors, indicating their leading positions in the scientific community. Journals with high impact factors are often perceived as more prestigious and of higher quality. Publishing in such journals can enhance the visibility and credibility of your research, as these journals are widely read and respected. Use the impact factor to compare journals within the same field.

It is important to note that impact factors vary across disciplines, so comparing journals from different fields based on impact factor alone can be misleading. For example, an impact factor of 5 might be high for a humanities journal but average for a medical journal. While useful, the impact factor should not be the sole criterion for choosing a journal. It does not account for the quality of individual articles, the peer review process, or the journal's overall editorial standards. Additionally, some journals may have high impact factors due to a few highly cited papers, skewing the average.

The reputation of a journal encompasses more than just its impact factor. It involves the journal's standing in the academic community, the quality of its published articles, and its influence on the field. Consider how long the journal has been in publication and its historical impact on the field. Established journals with a long history of publishing influential research often have strong reputations. Review the editorial board members and their affiliations. A prestigious editorial board often indicates rigorous peer review and high editorial standards. Editors who are leading experts in the field add credibility to the journal. Understand the journal's peer review process. High-quality journals typically have a rigorous and transparent review process, ensuring that only robust and well-conducted research is published. Look for feedback from both readers and authors. Positive testimonials from researchers who have published in the journal can provide insights into the submission process, editorial support, and overall experience. Similarly, reader feedback can highlight the journal's impact on the field.

Ensure the journal is indexed in major databases like PubMed, Web of Science, and Scopus. Being indexed in these databases increases the visibility and accessibility of the journal's articles, contributing to its reputation. Check if the journal is affiliated with reputable academic or professional organizations. Partnerships with such entities can enhance the journal's credibility and influence. Evaluate the journal's influence by examining how often its articles are cited in other works. Journals that frequently contribute to advancements in the field and are cited in seminal papers are generally held in high regard. Ensure the journal adheres to high ethical standards, including policies on plagiarism, conflicts of interest, and data integrity.

Journals associated with the Committee on Publication Ethics (COPE) (11) or similar organizations are committed to maintaining these standards. In summary, while the impact factor is an important metric for assessing a journal's influence, it should be considered alongside other factors that contribute to a journal's reputation. By evaluating both the impact factor and the overall reputation, you can select a journal that will maximize the visibility, credibility, and impact of your research.

PEER REVIEW PROCESS AND TIMELINE

The peer review process is essential in academic publishing, ensuring the integrity and reliability of research. Grasping its stages and timelines can significantly enhance an author's experience.

The Peer Review Process

Peer review involves experts evaluating a research manuscript thoroughly. The process starts with the manuscript's initial submission, followed by an editorial review. If the manuscript is suitable, it is sent to external reviewers for an in-depth evaluation. Based on their feedback, the editor decides whether to request revisions from the author or reject the manuscript. This cycle can repeat through multiple rounds before final acceptance and publication.

Understanding the Timeline

The duration of the peer review process varies widely, influenced by factors such as the journal, the research's complexity, and reviewers' availability.

Generally, the process includes the following stages:

Initial Submission and Editorial Assessment - This stage usually takes one to two weeks, during which the editorial team checks the manuscript for adherence to the journal's guidelines.

Reviewer Selection - Identifying and contacting suitable reviewers typically takes another one to two weeks.

Peer Review - Reviewers usually take four to six weeks to evaluate the manuscript and provide feedback.

Decision and Revisions - After receiving the reviewers' comments, the editor makes a decision. If revisions are required, the author may take several weeks to months to address the feedback and resubmit the manuscript.

Final Decision and Publication - Once all revisions are completed satisfactorily, the final decision is made. The production and proofreading stages may add several more weeks.

Some journals offer expedited review processes for urgent or time-sensitive research. Knowing these timelines helps authors manage their expectations and plan their research projects effectively.

PUBLICATION FEES

Understanding the financial aspects of publishing a research paper is essential. Publication fees, which can vary widely between journals, affect both the accessibility of your research and your budget.

Types of Publication Fees

Article Processing Charges - Common in open-access journals, the article processing charges cover costs related to peer review, publication, and online hosting. These fees can range from a few hundred to several thousand dollars.

Submission Fees - Some journals require a fee when you submit your manuscript, regardless of whether it is accepted. These fees typically cover administrative expenses.

Page Charges - Often found in print journals, page charges are based on the length of the article.

Color Figure Charges - Additional fees may be required for printing color images in print journals.

Supplementary Material Fees - Fees may apply for hosting additional data or content online.

Managing Publication Costs

To manage the financial burden of publication fees, consider the following strategies:

Fee Waivers and Discounts - Many journals offer waivers or discounts for authors who face financial difficulties.

Institutional Support - Some institutions provide coverage or reimbursement for publication fees incurred by their researchers.

Grant Funding - Include publication fees in your research grant applications to ensure they are covered.

Careful Journal Selection - Choose journals that align with your research goals while keeping the associated costs in mind. This balance will help ensure that your work is published without straining your budget.

CHAPTER 7.

SUBMITTING YOUR PAPER TO JOURNAL

Submitting your research paper to a journal involves a detailed and structured process that requires careful adherence to several key steps. It starts with thoroughly understanding the submission guidelines of the journal to ensure your manuscript meets all required criteria. Crafting an effective cover letter that succinctly conveys the importance and relevance of your research to the journal's audience is essential. Managing revisions and rejections professionally, responding constructively to feedback from editors and reviewers, and incorporating that feedback to improve your work are also critical components of the submission process. This guide will delve into each of these areas, offering practical tips to help you navigate the publication journey successfully. Table 7.1 presents a checklist for article submission to the target journal. Table 7.2 presents the checklist with additional questions to ask for each element of the checklist.

SUBMISSION GUIDELINES

Submitting your research paper to a journal involves several key aspects, including understanding submission guidelines, crafting a compelling cover letter, handling revisions and rejections, responding to editors and reviewers, and learning from feedback.

Understanding and Adhering to Submission Guidelines:

Every journal has specific submission guidelines that authors must follow to ensure their manuscript is considered for review. These guidelines typically include formatting requirements, word count limits, structure of the manuscript, and specific details on citations and references.

Manuscript Formatting - Ensure your paper adheres to the journal's formatting style, including font type and size, margins, line spacing, and section headings. Journals may provide templates to facilitate this process.

Structure and Content - Follow the journal's required structure, which usually includes sections such as the title, abstract, keywords, introduction, methods, results, discussion, conclusions, and references. Some journals may have additional sections like acknowledgments and conflicts of interest.

Citation Style - Use the citation style specified by the journal, such as APA, MLA, Chicago, or Harvard. Ensure consistency and accuracy in your references.

Supplementary Materials - If your research includes supplementary data, such as datasets, multimedia files, or additional documents, ensure these are prepared according to the journal's guidelines.

Ethical Considerations - Include statements on ethical approval, consent, and funding sources as required by the journal.

COVER LETTER ESSENTIALS

A well-structured cover letter is essential for effectively introducing your research to potential publishers. This document should concisely convey the manuscript's significance and its alignment with the journal's focus.

Begin by clearly stating the manuscript's title and type (e.g., original research, review article). Highlight the research's novelty, relevance to the target audience, and potential impact within the field. Justify the manuscript's suitability for the journal by referencing the journal's scope and how the research aligns with its objectives. Provide a brief overview of key findings and contributions. If applicable, include statements regarding ethical approval and any potential conflicts of interest. Conclude by offering contact information and expressing willingness to provide additional details.

HANDLING REVISIONS AND REJECTIONS

Handling revisions and rejections effectively is an essential skill for navigating the scientific publication process. It is important to approach this stage with a mindset focused on improvement and learning rather than seeing feedback as criticism.

RESPONDING TO REVISIONS

When revisions are requested, start by reading the reviewers' comments carefully. Review the feedback with an open mind, understanding that their goal is to improve the clarity, rigor, and contribution of your manuscript. Begin by categorizing the comments into major and minor changes:

- **Major changes** involve substantial revisions, such as reanalyzing data, clarifying arguments, or addressing gaps in your research. These should be prioritized because they have the most significant impact on the reviewers' decision.
- **Minor changes** often involve correcting typographical errors, adjusting formatting, or rephrasing certain parts for clarity. These are equally important but generally require less effort to implement.

Prepare a detailed response to each comment. For every suggested revision, explain what changes you made and where they can be found in the manuscript. For example, you might write, "As requested, we clarified the methodology section by adding details about the sampling procedure (p. 12, lines 34–40)." If a suggestion cannot be implemented, provide a polite and clear justification, such as, "We decided not to include additional data analysis as suggested, as the scope of the study was limited to [reason]."

When resubmitting your revised manuscript, include a "response to reviewers" document. This document is your opportunity to demonstrate professionalism, attention to detail, and a willingness to collaborate. Use it to systematically address each point raised, making it easy for reviewers to see how their feedback was incorporated. Highlight the changes in your manuscript either with tracked changes or by noting revisions in the text.

HANDLING REJECTIONS

Rejection is a normal part of the academic publishing process and happens to even the most experienced researchers. When a manuscript is rejected, take time to process the feedback before reacting. Reviewer comments can provide valuable insights into how your work is perceived by experts in the field.

Begin by understanding the reasons for rejection. Common reasons include:

- Misalignment with the journal's scope or audience.
- Insufficient novelty or significance of the study.
- Methodological flaws or incomplete analysis.
- Poorly written or structured manuscript.

Once you have identified the areas for improvement, decide on your next steps. If the feedback suggests that revisions could make the manuscript acceptable, consider revising and resubmitting to the same journal. A polite and detailed cover letter explaining how the manuscript has been improved can make a strong impression.

If resubmission to the same journal is not feasible or the feedback indicates fundamental issues, explore other journals that may be a better fit. Tailor your manuscript to the new journal's audience, format, and submission guidelines. This might include reframing your research question, reworking the introduction, or adding context to highlight its relevance to the new journal's readership.

PRO TIPS FOR STUDENTS

- **Stay positive** - Rejections are not a reflection of your worth as a researcher but an opportunity to grow and improve your work.
- **Be proactive** - Use feedback constructively. Even harsh criticism can guide you toward a stronger and more impactful paper.
- **Seek mentorship** - If you are unsure how to address specific comments, seek advice from colleagues, mentors, or co-authors who may have more experience in responding to reviewer feedback.
- **Track your submissions** - Maintain a record of where you have submitted your manuscript, along with reviewer comments, so you can track progress and refine your strategy.

Handling revisions and rejections effectively not only increases your chances of publishing successfully but also builds essential skills for long-term success in academia. Each cycle of revision and resubmission is an opportunity to refine your research, strengthen your writing, and develop resilience.

RESPONDING TO EDITORS AND REVIEWERS

Responding to editors and reviewers is one of the most critical stages in the publication process. The way authors handle this step can significantly influence the outcome of their submission. Successful responses demonstrate professionalism, attention to detail, and a willingness to collaborate to improve the quality of the manuscript.

START WITH GRATITUDE AND RESPECT

Begin your response letter by thanking the reviewers and editors for their time and effort in providing feedback. Acknowledge the value of their comments in helping to refine your work. For instance, you might open with: "We would like to thank the reviewers for their thoughtful and detailed feedback, which has been invaluable in improving our manuscript."

This sets a positive tone and reflects your appreciation for their role in the publication process.

STRUCTURE YOUR RESPONSE CLEARLY

Organize your response into a systematic and easy-to-follow format. A common approach is to use a table or numbered list, addressing each reviewer's comment individually.

1. **Restate the Comment** - Begin by briefly restating the reviewer's suggestion or critique. This shows that you have understood their concern and ensures clarity.
2. **Describe Your Revision** - Explain what changes you made to address the comment. Be specific, citing the exact location of the revision in the manuscript (e.g., "We have clarified this point in the introduction, p. 3, lines 14–18").
3. **Provide a Justification if Necessary** - If you choose not to implement a suggestion, provide a clear, evidence-based explanation. For example, "We decided not to include additional data analysis as suggested because the scope of our study is limited to [specific reason]. However, we have acknowledged this limitation in the discussion section, p. 12, lines 22–25."

Where possible, use bold text or color coding to differentiate reviewer comments, your responses, and manuscript revisions. This visual clarity makes it easier for reviewers to track the changes.

MAINTAIN A PROFESSIONAL TONE

Throughout your response, maintain a respectful and professional tone, even if you disagree with a reviewer's comment. Avoid emotional language or dismissive phrasing. Instead of saying, "The reviewer is mistaken," try, "We appreciate the reviewer's perspective; however, we believe the original approach is appropriate because [reason]."

Remember, reviewers are experts in your field who volunteer their time to help improve your manuscript. Engaging with their comments thoughtfully and diplomatically builds a positive relationship and reflects well on you as an author.

ADDRESS ALL COMMENTS, BIG OR SMALL

Reviewers typically provide a mix of major and minor comments. Address every comment, even seemingly trivial ones, to demonstrate thoroughness. For minor suggestions like typos or formatting issues, simply state, "This has been corrected as suggested."

For major comments, take the time to make meaningful revisions. Highlight how these changes improve the manuscript, aligning with the reviewer's suggestions.

RESPOND TO EDITOR-SPECIFIC COMMENTS

Editors often provide overarching feedback or identify specific concerns that reviewers might not have mentioned. Treat these comments with equal importance, as the editor has the final say in accepting or rejecting the manuscript. Show how you have addressed their concerns directly and clearly in your response.

ANTICIPATE FOLLOW-UP QUESTIONS

Sometimes, addressing a comment might raise additional questions. When revising your manuscript, ensure that your changes are comprehensive and do not create new ambiguities. For example, if you add new data or clarify a method, make sure it aligns seamlessly with the rest of the manuscript.

CONCLUDE POSITIVELY

End your response letter by reiterating your gratitude and expressing your willingness to make further revisions if needed. For example: "We sincerely thank the reviewers and editors for their constructive feedback. We hope the revised manuscript meets the standards of the journal and are happy to provide further clarification or revisions if required."

TIPS FOR STUDENTS

- **Take Time to Reflect** - After receiving feedback, give yourself time to process it calmly before drafting your response. This helps you approach comments with a clear and constructive mindset.
- **Seek Input** - If you are unsure about how to respond to specific comments, discuss them with mentors, co-authors, or colleagues who may provide helpful insights.
- **Be Thorough** - Ensure no comment is overlooked. Even minor feedback can contribute to improving your manuscript's quality.
- **Stay Organized** - Use a template or checklist to ensure you address every comment systematically.

By responding to editors and reviewers effectively, you demonstrate your commitment to producing high quality research and your respect for the publication process. This not only increases the likelihood of acceptance but also establishes you as a professional and collaborative researcher.

LEARNING FROM FEEDBACK

Feedback from reviewers and editors is an invaluable tool for refining your manuscript and advancing your skills as a researcher. It is essential to approach this feedback with an open and constructive mindset, seeing it as an opportunity to enhance your work rather than as criticism.

TREATING FEEDBACK AS A LEARNING OPPORTUNITY

Feedback reflects how your research is perceived by experts. By addressing their comments, you can improve the clarity, depth, and rigor of your work. Focus on recurring themes in their suggestions, as these often highlight critical areas for improvement, such as methodology, analysis, or presentation. Use these insights not only to refine the current manuscript but also to strengthen your practices in future projects.

GAINING INSIGHTS INTO METHODOLOGY AND WRITING

Comments on your methods or analyses provide valuable lessons on research design and statistical interpretation, while feedback on clarity, structure, and adherence to journal guidelines can enhance your communication skills. Implement these suggestions to improve both the quality of your manuscript and your understanding of field-specific standards.

APPLYING FEEDBACK BEYOND THE CURRENT MANUSCRIPT

Reviewer feedback offers long-term benefits by highlighting patterns in your work. For example, repeated comments about insufficient detail in methods or weak argumentation can guide you to focus on these areas in future research. Maintain a checklist of lessons learned to streamline your writing process and align with journal expectations in the future.

EMBRACING RESILIENCE

Feedback can be challenging, especially when revisions are extensive, or critiques target fundamental aspects of your research. Stay resilient, process comments calmly, and seek advice from mentors if needed.

Remember, every researcher faces critical reviews, and learning from these experiences builds stronger, more impactful scholarship.

Ultimately, feedback is a tool for growth, helping you improve your current manuscript while building skills that will strengthen your future research contributions.

Table 7.1. Article Submission Checklist

Step	Task	Check
Pre-Submission Preparation		
	Identify Appropriate Journal	[ ]
	Understand Submission Guidelines	[ ]
Manuscript Preparation		
	Format manuscript according to guidelines	[ ]
	Include all required sections	[ ]
	Prepare supplementary materials	[ ]
	Include ethical considerations	[ ]
Cover Letter		
	State manuscript title and type	[ ]
	Highlight research significance	[ ]
	Justify fit with the journal	[ ]
	Summarize key findings	[ ]
	Include ethical statements and contact information	[ ]
Submission Process		
	Register/log in to submission system	[ ]
	Fill in manuscript and author details	[ ]
	Upload manuscript and supplementary materials	[ ]
	Review and confirm submission	[ ]
Post-Submission		
	Verify receipt of confirmation email	[ ]
	Track submission status	[ ]
	Respond to additional information requests promptly	[ ]
Handling Revisions and Rejections		
	Read editor's and reviewers' comments carefully	[ ]
	Prioritize and address major revisions first	[ ]
	Prepare detailed response document	[ ]
	Revise manuscript according to feedback	[ ]
	Highlight changes in revised manuscript	[ ]
	Upload revised manuscript and response document	[ ]
	Review feedback after rejection	[ ]
	Consider revising and resubmitting	[ ]
Responding to Feedback		
	Thank reviewers for their comments	[ ]
	Address each comment individually	[ ]
	Provide clear and evidence-based responses	[ ]
Learning from Feedback		

Identify recurring themes in feedback	[ ]
Use feedback to improve current and future research	[ ]
Incorporate methodological and presentation suggestions	[ ]

Table 7.2. Article Submission Checklist with Relevant Questions

Element	Relevant Questions
Journal Selection	- What is the scope of the journal? - What is the journal's impact factor? - Who is the journal's target audience? - What is the journal's acceptance rate? - What is the journal's publication timeline? - Does the journal have any special issues related to your topic?
Manuscript Preparation	- Have you followed the journal's manuscript guidelines? - Is your manuscript well-structured and cohesive? - Are all sections properly formatted? - Have you proofread the manuscript for language and grammar? - Are all necessary supplementary materials prepared?
Literature Review	- Have you included the most recent and relevant sources? - Is your literature review comprehensive and well-organized? - Have you identified gaps in the current literature? - How does your research build on existing studies? - Have you critically analyzed the sources?
Abstract and Title	- Does your title reflect the main finding or purpose of your research? - Does your abstract summarize the key points? - Is your abstract within the word limit specified by the journal? - Does the abstract include keywords for search optimization?
Introduction and Background	- Does your introduction clearly state the research problem? - Is the background linked to your research objectives? - Have you provided a rationale for your study? - Are the key terms and concepts clearly defined? - Have you outlined the structure of your paper?
Methods and Results	- Are your research methods described in enough detail for reproducibility? - Are your results presented clearly? - Have you justified your methodological choices? - Are there any potential biases in your methods? - Have you included all relevant data in your results?
Discussion and Conclusion	- Have you interpreted your results accurately? - Do your conclusions summarize the key findings and their implications? - Have you discussed the limitations of your study? - Have you suggested areas for future research? - How do your findings contribute to the field?
Figures and Tables	- Are your figures and tables clear and informative? - Are they well-integrated into the manuscript? - Are all figures and tables referenced in the text? - Do the captions adequately describe the content of the figures and tables?

	- Are your visuals in the correct format for the journal?
Revising and Editing	- Have you revised for clarity and coherence? - Have you sought feedback from peers? - Have you checked for consistency in terminology and style? - Have you removed any redundant information? - Have you used software tools to check for errors?
Submission Process	- Have you written a compelling cover letter? - Have you adhered to the submission guidelines? - Is your manuscript formatted according to the journal's requirements? - Have you included all required documents (e.g., ethical approvals, supplementary files)? - Have you created an account on the journal's submission platform?
Peer Review	- Do you understand the peer review process? - Are you prepared to respond constructively to feedback? - Have you drafted responses to potential reviewer comments? - Have you revised the manuscript based on internal feedback? - Are you ready to make additional revisions if needed?
Dealing with Rejections	- How can you use the feedback to improve your manuscript? - What alternative journals can you consider? - Have you discussed the feedback with your co-authors? - What steps will you take to address the reviewers' concerns? - How will you stay motivated after a rejection?
Promoting Published Work	- How will you promote your research on social media? - Which academic networks and conferences can you engage with? - Have you prepared a press release or summary for broader audiences? - Have you updated your professional profiles with the new publication? - What strategies will you use to engage with the research community?
Ethical Considerations	- Are all sources properly cited? - Have you used plagiarism detection tools? - Are authorship contributions clear? - Have you obtained all necessary ethical approvals? - Have you disclosed any potential conflicts of interest? - Are you adhering to the ethical guidelines of the journal?

CHAPTER 8.

BEYOND PUBLICATION

In the academic world, publishing your research is just the first step. To make a lasting impact, your work must be shared, discussed, and utilized by peers and experts in your field. Effective promotion is essential—it is the way your research reaches those who can truly benefit from it. Networking, attending conferences, and utilizing social media platforms are powerful avenues for extending your work's reach beyond the confines of academic journals. These efforts not only boost the visibility of your research but also pave the way for new opportunities and collaborations.

Promoting your work is also integral to building a robust research profile. Keeping your CV updated and committing to continuous learning are crucial for maintaining relevance in a rapidly changing academic environment. By actively engaging in promoting your research and investing in your professional growth, you ensure that your contributions are recognized and that your career continues to flourish.

Promoting Your Work

After your paper is published, the journey does not end. Promoting your research is crucial to ensuring it reaches the widest possible audience and has the maximum impact. Here are practical steps and strategies for effectively promoting your work:

Networking and Conferences

Networking and attending conferences are essential for building your professional reputation and disseminating your research.

Attend Relevant Conferences:

Identify Key Conferences - Look for conferences that align with your research field.

Prepare Your Presentation - Develop a clear and engaging presentation of your research findings.

Engage with Attendees - Network with other researchers, attend sessions, and participate in discussions.

Distribute Copies - Bring printed copies or digital access details of your paper to share with interested colleagues.

Join Professional Organizations:

Membership - Become a member of relevant academic and professional organizations.

Participate Actively - Get involved in committees, special interest groups, and attend workshops.

Present Your Work - Take opportunities to present your research at organization meetings.

Collaborate and Follow Up:

Collaborate: Explore potential collaborations with other researchers you meet.

Follow Up - Maintain connections by following up with new contacts after the conference.

Social Media and Research Gateways

Utilize social media and research platforms to promote your work and connect with the global research community.

Social Media Platforms:

Twitter - Share key findings, link to your paper, and use relevant hashtags to increase visibility.

LinkedIn - Post about your publication and engage with professional groups.

Facebook - Join academic groups and share your research within these communities.

Research Gateways:

ResearchGate - Upload your paper, engage with other researchers, and follow relevant topics.

Academia.edu - Share your research, track its impact, and connect with peers.

Google Scholar - Ensure your profile is up-to-date and includes your latest publications.

Personal Website and Blogs:

Create a Website - Develop a personal academic website showcasing your research, CV, and publications.

Write Blog Posts - Write blog posts summarizing your research in an accessible way for a broader audience.

Building a Research Profile

Building and maintaining a robust research profile is essential for your academic career. It helps you track your progress, showcase your achievements, and stay updated in your field.

Maintaining an Updated CV

Keep your CV up-to-date to reflect your latest academic achievements and research activities.

Regular Updates:

> *Add New Publications* - Include all recent publications and presentations.

> *Highlight Awards* - List any awards, grants, or recognitions received.

Detail Teaching Experience - Include courses taught and any teaching-related activities.

Format and Structure:

Clear Sections - Organize your CV into sections such as Education, Research Experience, Publications, and Professional Activities.

Consistent Formatting - Use consistent formatting and style throughout your CV.

Tailor for Opportunities - Customize your CV to highlight relevant experiences for specific job applications or grant proposals.

Professional Profiles:

Online Presence - Keep your professional profiles (e.g., LinkedIn, ResearchGate) aligned with your CV.

Profile Picture - Use a professional photo across all profiles.

Continuous Learning and Development

Engage in continuous learning to stay current in your field and enhance your skills.

Attend Workshops and Seminars:

Skill Development - Participate in workshops and seminars that offer training in new research methods, statistical tools, or writing skills.

Stay Updated - Attend seminars and webinars on the latest developments in your field.

Enroll in Courses:

Advanced Courses - Take online or in-person courses related to your research area or new methodologies.

Certifications - Obtain certifications that can enhance your expertise and add value to your CV.

Read Widely:

Journal Subscriptions - Subscribe to key journals in your field.

Stay Informed - Regularly read articles, books, and reviews to stay informed about new research trends and findings.

Engage with Mentors:

Seek Guidance - Maintain relationships with mentors who can provide advice and feedback.

Peer Discussions - Participate in discussion groups or journal clubs to engage with peers on current research topics.

CHAPTER 9.

ARTIFICIAL INTELLIGENCE ETHICAL USE IN WRITING

Tools like ChatGPT and Claude, powered by large language models, have the potential to revolutionize the writing and publication process in scientific research. When used appropriately and ethically, ChatGPT can be of great assistance to researchers in generating ideas, structuring content, and refining their manuscripts, making the writing process more efficient and effective. By making use of such technologies, researchers can enhance their productivity and ensure their work meets the highest standards of academic integrity.

OVERVIEW OF AI AND CHATGPT

Artificial Intelligence refers to the development of computer systems that can perform tasks typically requiring human intelligence (12). These tasks include learning from data, reasoning to make decisions, and self-correction over time. Artificial Intelligence encompasses a broad spectrum of technologies, from basic algorithms to sophisticated neural networks capable of complex analyses. Among these technologies, ChatGPT, created by OpenAI, is a notable advanced language model. Using the Generative Pre-trained Transformer (GPT) architecture, ChatGPT processes and generates text that is both contextually relevant and coherent.

By analyzing extensive datasets, ChatGPT can engage in meaningful conversations, answer queries, and assist with various writing tasks. Its proficiency in understanding and generating human language makes it a versatile tool for academic writing, where precision and clarity are paramount.

Applications in Academic Writing

ChatGPT offers substantial benefits for academic writing, helping generate ideas, structure content, and draft text sections. It supports researchers and students by overcoming writer's block, improving argument clarity, and ensuring appropriate language usage for academic contexts. Specific applications include:

- *Idea Generation* - ChatGPT assists in brainstorming research topics and generating innovative ideas for exploration, providing a fresh perspective, and suggesting relevant themes.
- *Outlining and Structuring* - It helps create logical and coherent outlines for papers, ensuring each section builds upon the previous one effectively.
- *Drafting Text* - ChatGPT can produce initial drafts for sections like introductions, literature reviews, and conclusions, serving as a foundation for further development.
- *Editing and Refinement* - It suggests language, style, and clarity improvements, assisting in refining drafts for better readability and impact.
- *Summarization* - ChatGPT can condense large volumes of text, aiding in literature synthesis and abstract preparation.

Using ChatGPT ethically is crucial to maintaining the integrity and originality of academic work. AI should complement human creativity and critical thinking rather than replace them.

ETHICAL CONSIDERATIONS IN USING CHATGPT

Understanding AI Ethics

AI ethics involves the principles and guidelines that govern the responsible use of AI technologies. These include ensuring that AI does not harm individuals or society and is used transparently and fairly. Key aspects include:

- **Transparency** - Clearly explain how AI systems operate and make decisions, ensuring users understand AI's role and capabilities.
- **Fairness** - Strive to eliminate biases that could lead to unfair treatment of individuals or groups, promoting equality and inclusivity.
- **Accountability** - Hold developers and users accountable for AI system outcomes, taking responsibility for their impact.
- **Privacy** - Protect user data and respect privacy, ensuring data is used ethically and securely.

Understanding these principles is essential for the ethical use of ChatGPT in academic writing.

Responsibilities of the User

Users of ChatGPT have a duty to uphold ethical standards in their usage of the tool. This involves acknowledging the AI's limitations, responsibly using AI-generated content, and maintaining academic integrity. Responsibilities include:

- **Critical Evaluation** - Thoroughly review AI-generated content to ensure it meets academic standards and is accurate and relevant.
- **Supplementary Use** - Use ChatGPT as a complementary tool, enhancing but not replacing human judgment and creativity.
- **Integrity** - Ensure the final work remains original, and properly acknowledge AI assistance.

Transparency and Disclosure

Acknowledging AI Assistance

Disclosing the use of AI tools like ChatGPT in academic content creation is essential. This transparency recognizes the AI's contributions and prevents misrepresentation of the work's originality. Acknowledgment can be included in the paper's acknowledgments section or as a footnote, detailing the extent of AI involvement. For instance:

"This research utilized ChatGPT, a language model by OpenAI, for drafting sections of the introduction and literature review."

Proper Attribution Practices

Giving credit for AI-generated content where due is crucial for maintaining transparency. If ChatGPT significantly contributed to the research or writing process, it should be acknowledged appropriately, reflecting the collaborative nature of the work. This practice ensures academic honesty and integrity.

Plagiarism and Originality

Ensuring Original Work

While ChatGPT can aid in text generation, it is the user's responsibility to ensure the final work is original. This involves critically reviewing and revising AI-generated content to align with personal insights and research findings. Directly copying AI-generated text without modification and engagement is unethical. Users must ensure their work reflects their own analysis and understanding.

Avoiding Unintentional Plagiarism

Unintentional plagiarism can occur if AI-generated text is used without proper modification or citation. To avoid this, users should review and edit content from ChatGPT thoroughly, integrating it seamlessly and ethically into their work. Proper citation and acknowledgment of AI assistance are critical to maintaining academic integrity.

Data Privacy and Confidentiality

Protecting Sensitive Information

Users must ensure that any sensitive or confidential information used with ChatGPT is adequately protected. This includes avoiding the input of personal data or proprietary information into the AI system to prevent compromising data privacy. Awareness of the data shared and steps to safeguard it are essential.

Ethical Use of User Data

Understanding how user data is processed and stored when using AI tools is crucial. Users should ensure that their data is handled ethically and that the AI tool complies with relevant data protection regulations, such as GDPR or CCPA. Familiarity with AI tools' privacy policies is necessary for ethical use.

Accuracy and Reliability

Verifying AI-Generated Content

AI-generated content should always be verified for accuracy. Users should cross-check facts, data, and references provided by ChatGPT to ensure correctness and reliability. AI can generate plausible but incorrect information, making verification a critical step to maintain the credibility of academic work.

Cross-Checking Facts and Data

Maintaining the reliability of academic work requires cross-checking all AI-generated facts and data against trusted sources. This practice helps prevent the dissemination of false information and maintains the credibility of the academic work. Cross-referencing with peer-reviewed articles, official reports, and other reliable sources is essential.

Bias and Fairness

Recognizing and Mitigating Bias in AI

AI models such as ChatGPT can inadvertently perpetuate biases present in the training data. Users should be aware of this possibility and actively work to identify and mitigate biases in AI-generated content. This involves critically evaluating the content and making necessary adjustments to ensure fairness. Awareness of potential biases and steps to address them are crucial for ethical AI use.

Ensuring Fair Representation

Fair representation involves accurately and equitably representing all groups and perspectives in academic writing. Users should strive to include diverse viewpoints and avoid perpetuating stereotypes or biased narratives. Ensuring inclusivity and fairness in AI-generated content promotes ethical writing practices.

Limitations of ChatGPT

Understanding the AI's Boundaries

Users must understand ChatGPT's limitations. While it can generate human-like text, it lacks full comprehension of context and may not always produce accurate or contextually appropriate content. Recognizing these boundaries helps users utilize ChatGPT more effectively and ethically. Awareness of limitations allows for appropriate use of AI tools.

Complementing AI with Human Judgment

AI-generated content should always be complemented with human judgment. Users should critically assess and revise AI outputs, ensuring the final work reflects human insight and scholarly rigor. Combining AI assistance with human expertise ensures that academic standards are maintained.

Best Practices for Ethical Use

Guidelines for Responsible AI Use

Responsible AI use involves adhering to ethical guidelines and best practices. This includes transparency, proper attribution, content verification, and maintaining the originality and integrity of the work. Users should stay informed about AI ethics and continuously evaluate their AI tool usage. Adhering to best practices ensures ethical and effective AI use.

Examples of Ethical Writing with AI Assistance

- *Scenario 1* - A student uses ChatGPT to generate an outline for their research paper. They then develop each section based on their research, modifying and expanding AI-generated suggestions with their insights.
- *Scenario 2* - A researcher uses ChatGPT to draft a literature review. They critically review the generated text, verify all sources, and rewrite sections to ensure accuracy and originality before including it in their paper.
- *Scenario 3* - An academic uses ChatGPT to refine the language and structure of their manuscript. They acknowledge the use of AI in their acknowledgments, ensuring transparency.

CHAPTER 10.

PUBLICATION PROCESS CANVAS

The Publication Process Canvas is a thorough guide aimed at helping researchers, especially those new to the field, successfully navigate the complex process of writing and publishing scientific papers (Table 10.1). It breaks down the publication journey into clear, manageable steps, providing detailed descriptions and actionable advice for each stage.

From selecting an appropriate journal to promoting your published research, this canvas addresses every essential phase. It highlights the importance of careful preparation, adherence to ethical standards, and effective presentation of research findings. By following this structured approach, researchers can improve the quality of their manuscripts, increase their chances of acceptance, and boost the visibility and impact of their work.

Each component of the canvas is designed to offer practical guidance and support, making the challenging process of academic publishing more approachable. Whether you are drafting your first manuscript or seeking to enhance your publication strategy, the Expanded Publication Process Canvas delivers valuable insights and strategies to help you thrive in the competitive academic landscape.

Figure 10.1 presents a visual representation of the Publication Process Canvas.

Table 10.1. Publication Process Canvas

Element	Description	Tips
Journal Selection	Strategies for selecting the most suitable journal for your research. Evaluate the journal's scope, impact factor, and target audience.	- Use journal finder tools provided by publishers. - Seek recommendations from colleagues and mentors. - Review recent issues of the journal to understand its focus.
Manuscript Preparation	Comprehensive steps for preparing your manuscript, including clear structuring, adherence to journal guidelines, and effective writing techniques.	- Use manuscript templates if provided by the journal. - Ensure all sections are cohesive and well-integrated.
Literature Review	Guidelines for conducting a thorough literature review to contextualize your research. Ensure citations of relevant and recent sources.	- Use reference management software (e.g., EndNote, Zotero). - Create an annotated bibliography to organize your sources.
Abstract and Title	Techniques for crafting a compelling title and abstract that accurately represent your paper's content and attract readers' attention.	- Use active voice and precise language. - Ensure the abstract stands alone and provides a comprehensive overview.
Introduction and Background	How to write a strong introduction that sets the context for your research, including a comprehensive background and literature review.	- Ensure the introduction is engaging and informative. - Link the background to your research questions and objectives.
Methods and Results	Detailed description of your research methods and clear presentation of results. Use figures and tables to enhance clarity and understanding.	- Ensure reproducibility by including sufficient detail in the methods section. - Use visuals to complement and clarify the text.
Discussion and Conclusion	Interpreting your results and discussing their implications. Summarize key findings in a concise	- Avoid overstating your conclusions. - Relate your findings to broader research and practical applications.

	and impactful conclusion.	
Figures and Tables	Best practices for creating clear, informative figures and tables. Ensure they are well-integrated and enhance the manuscript's readability.	- Use consistent formatting for all visuals. - Include captions that provide context and explanations.
Revising and Editing	Techniques for effectively revising and editing your manuscript. Seek peer feedback and make necessary improvements.	- Use editing tools (e.g., Grammarly) to catch errors. - Take breaks between revisions to gain a fresh perspective.
Submission Process	Step-by-step guide for submitting your manuscript. Includes tips for writing a cover letter and adhering to submission guidelines.	- Double-check all submission requirements. - Keep a copy of all submitted documents.
Peer Review	Understanding the peer review process. Learn how to respond to reviewers' comments constructively and make necessary revisions.	- Respond professionally to reviewers' comments. - Revise the manuscript thoroughly based on feedback.
Dealing with Rejections	Strategies for handling manuscript rejections positively. Utilize feedback to improve and resubmit your work.	- Keep a list of potential alternative journals. - Seek support from colleagues and mentors.
Promoting Published Work	Tips for increasing your research's visibility post-publication. Leverage social media, academic networks, and conferences.	- Create a summary of your research for wider audiences. - Collaborate with your institution's press office for broader reach.
Ethical Considerations	Address ethical issues such as plagiarism, authorship disputes, and maintaining research integrity. Ensure adherence to ethical standards.	- Familiarize yourself with the journal's ethical guidelines. - Use plagiarism detection software to check your manuscript.

FIGURE 10.1. PUBLICATION PROCESS CANVAS

METHODS AND RESULTS

Detailed description of your research methods and clear presentation of results. Use figures and tables to enhance clarity and understanding.

DISCUSSION AND CONCLUSION

Interpreting your results and discussing their implications. Summarize key findings in a concise and impactful conclusion.

JOURNAL SELECTION

Strategies for selecting the most suitable journal for your research. Evaluate the journal's scope, impact factor, and target audience.

MANUSCRIPT PREPARATION

Comprehensive steps for preparing your manuscript, including clear structuring, adherence to journal guidelines, and effective writing techniques.

INTRODUCTION AND BACKGROUND

How to write a strong introduction that sets the context for your research, including a comprehensive background and literature review.

SUBMISSION PROCESS

Step-by-step guide for submitting your manuscript. Includes tips for writing a cover letter and adhering to submission guidelines.

FIGURES AND TABLES

Best practices for creating clear, informative figures and tables. Ensure they are well-integrated and enhance the manuscript's readability.

LITERATURE REVIEW

Guidelines for conducting a thorough literature review to contextualize your research. Ensure citations of relevant and recent sources.

ABSTRACT AND TITLE

Techniques for crafting a compelling title and abstract that accurately represent your paper's content and attract readers' attention.

REVISING AND EDITING

Techniques for effectively revising and editing your manuscript. Seek peer feedback and make necessary improvements.

PEER REVIEW

Understanding the peer review process. Learn how to respond to reviewers' comments constructively and make necessary revisions.

DEALING WITH REJECTIONS

Strategies for handling manuscript rejections positively. Utilize feedback to improve and resubmit your work.

PROMOTING PUBLISHED WORK

Tips for increasing your research's visibility post-publication. Leverage social media, academic networks, and conferences.

ETHICAL CONSIDERATIONS

Address ethical issues such as plagiarism, authorship disputes, and maintaining research integrity. Ensure adherence to ethical standards.

STEP-BY-STEP GUIDE TO USING THE EXPANDED PUBLICATION PROCESS CANVAS

The Expanded Publication Process Canvas is a strategic tool designed to guide researchers, writers, and academics through the complex journey of publishing scholarly work. It serves as a comprehensive roadmap that demystifies each step of the publication process, ensuring clarity, organization, and efficiency from start to finish. Whether you are a first-time author or an experienced researcher, the canvas helps streamline the process, reducing stress and enhancing the quality of your work.

WHY USE THE CANVAS?

Publishing a scientific manuscript can be a daunting task, involving multiple steps and meticulous attention to detail. The canvas offers a structured approach that helps you navigate this journey systematically, ensuring that nothing is overlooked. Here is why the canvas is useful:

1. **Clarity and Organization** - The canvas breaks down the entire publication process into manageable, clearly defined components. By addressing one element at a time, you can focus your efforts and stay organized.
2. **Comprehensive Coverage** - It addresses every stage of publication, from journal selection and manuscript preparation to peer review and post-publication promotion. Each element is accompanied by guiding questions and actionable tips, making it easier to proceed with confidence.
3. **Efficiency and Productivity** - With its structured format, the canvas helps you stay on track, minimizing delays and optimizing your workflow. By using the canvas, you can allocate your time and resources effectively.
4. **Quality Enhancement** - The guiding questions embedded in each section encourage critical reflection, improving the rigor and coherence of your manuscript. The canvas promotes best practices that elevate the overall quality of your work.
5. **Ethical Compliance** - The canvas emphasizes ethical considerations, such as proper citation, authorship, and research

integrity, helping you navigate these critical aspects with confidence.

How the Canvas Works

The canvas is divided into key elements that correspond to the essential steps of the publication process. Each element includes descriptions, guiding questions, and practical tips tailored to help you navigate that specific stage. The framework is designed to be iterative, meaning you can revisit elements as needed, ensuring continuous improvement.

What Does the Canvas Cover?

1. **Journal Selection** - Strategies for identifying and evaluating journals to find the best fit for your research.
2. **Manuscript Preparation** - Step-by-step guidance for structuring, writing, and formatting your manuscript.
3. **Literature Review** - Tips for conducting a thorough review to contextualize your research.
4. **Abstract and Title** - Techniques for crafting compelling titles and abstracts that capture attention.
5. **Introduction and Background** - Guidelines for setting the context and framing your research question.
6. **Methods and Results** - Best practices for detailing your methodology and presenting findings clearly.
7. **Discussion and Conclusion** - How to interpret your results and link them to broader implications.
8. **Figures and Tables (Visual Elements)** - Advice for creating impactful figures and tables.
9. **Revising and Editing** - Tools and techniques for polishing your manuscript.
10. **Submission Process** - Instructions for adhering to submission guidelines and preparing cover letters.
11. **Peer Review** - Insights into the review process and how to respond constructively to feedback.
12. **Dealing with Rejections** - Strategies for improving your manuscript and resubmitting elsewhere.
13. **Promoting Published Work** - Tips for increasing visibility and impact after publication.
14. **Ethical Considerations** - A checklist for ensuring compliance with research and publication ethics.

How to Begin with the Canvas

The canvas is designed to be simple yet powerful. Here is how to get started:

1. **Access the Canvas -** Print or save a digital copy to use as your working guide.
2. **Understand Each Element -** Take time to read through the descriptions and questions for each element. Familiarize yourself with the flow of the process.
3. **Integrate into Your Workflow -** Use the canvas as your checklist or brainstorming tool at every stage of manuscript preparation and publication.

CHAPTER 11.

TOOLS AND RESOURCES

Navigating the process of writing and publishing a scientific paper is much smoother with the proper tools and resources. This chapter offers vital templates and worksheets to simplify manuscript preparation, revision strategies, and cover letter writing. Additionally, we will introduce various software and online tools to support writing, managing references, and organizing projects.

LITERATURE REVIEW CHECKLIST (PRISMA CHECKLIST)

Step		Task	Check
Title	1	Highlight the report as a literature review	[ ]
ABSTRACT			
Abstract	2	A structured summary	[ ]
INTRODUCTION			
Rationale	3	Rationale for the literature review	[ ]
Objectives	4	Explicitly state question(s) or objective(s)	[ ]
METHODS			
Eligibility criteria	5	Exclusion and inclusion criteria of literature review	[ ]
Information sources	6	Electronic databases, websites, organisations, registers, reference lists etc., (with dates last searched)	[ ]
Search strategy	7	List the full search strategy for each database, registers and websites, including any filters and limits used.	[ ]
Selection process	8	Details about how studies fulfilled the exclusion and inclusion criteria of the literature review	[ ]
Data collection process	9	How data was collected from studies (including how reviewers were involved)	[ ]
Data items	10a	Elements for which data were sought	[ ]
	10b	Elements for which data were extracted	[ ]
Study risk of bias assessment	11	Assessment of bias risk	[ ]
Effect measures	12	Highlight for each variable the effect measure(s) used in the results synthesis	[ ]
RESULTS			
Study selection	13a	Search results and process of selection (records using PRISMA flow chart diagram)	[ ]
	13b	Cite studies meeting inclusion criteria	[ ]
Study characteristics	14	Study characteristics.	[ ]
Results of syntheses	15	Summarise characteristics and risk of bias	[ ]
Reporting	16	Bias risk assessment for each synthesis	[ ]

biases			
Certainty of evidence	17	Confidence in the body of evidence	[ ]
DISCUSSION			
Discussion	18	Explanation of the results in in relation to other literature	[ ]
	19	Weaknesses of the evidence	[ ]
	20	Limitations of processes used in literature review	[ ]
	21	Discussion practical, policy and research implications of results	[ ]

Distributed under the terms of the Creative Commons Attribution License From: Page MJ, McKenzie JE, Bossuyt PM, Boutron I, Hoffmann TC, Mulrow CD, et al. The PRISMA 2020 statement: an updated guideline for reporting systematic reviews (13).

RESEARCH PUBLICATION CHECKLIST

Step	Task	Checklist	Check
Chapter 2: Understanding Scientific Papers	Importance of Publishing	- Understand why publishing research is important	[ ]
	Overview of the Publishing Process	- Learn the high-level steps of the publication process from start to finish	[ ]
	The Structure of a Scientific Paper	- Write the Abstract - Develop the Introduction - Detail the Methods - Present the Results - Write the Discussion - Summarize in the Conclusion - Create the References section - Include Appendices (if any)	[ ] [ ] [ ] [ ] [ ] [ ] [ ] [ ]
	Types of Scientific Papers	- Identify if your paper is an Original Research Article - Determine if it is a Review Article - Consider if it is a Case Report - Check if it is a Short Communication - Decide if it is an Opinion Paper	[ ] [ ] [ ] [ ] [ ]
	Ethics in Scientific Writing	- Avoid plagiarism - Define authorship and contribution - Disclose conflicts of interest	[ ] [ ] [ ]
Chapter 3: Preparing to Write the Manuscript	Choosing a Research Topic	- Identify gaps in the literature - Align with your research interests	[ ] [ ]
	Literature Review	- Conduct effective searches - Synthesize information - Organize sources systematically	[ ] [ ] [ ]
	Formulating Research Questions and Hypotheses	- Ensure clarity and precision - Develop testable hypotheses - Ensure relevance	[ ] [ ] [ ]
	Choosing the Right Journal	- Select the most appropriate journal for your research - Understand journal requirements - Read and interpret author guidelines	[ ] [ ] [ ]
	Structuring Your Paper	- Follow detailed guidance on structuring the paper (Introduction, Methods, Results, Discussion)	[ ]

Chapter 4: Writing the Paper	Writing the Abstract	- Summarize the study - Include key elements	[ ] [ ]
	Crafting the Introduction	- Provide background information - State the problem - Outline objectives and hypotheses	[ ] [ ] [ ]
	Describing the Methods	- Detail procedures - Justify methodological choices - Ensure reproducibility	[ ] [ ] [ ]
	Presenting the Results	- Present data clearly and concisely - Use tables and figures effectively	[ ] [ ]
	Discussing the Findings	- Interpret results - Compare with existing literature - Discuss limitations and future directions	[ ] [ ] [ ]
	Writing the Conclusion	- Summarize key findings - Discuss implications and recommendations	[ ] [ ]
	Citing Sources and Creating References	- Use proper citation styles - Manage references systematically	[ ] [ ]
Chapter 5: Refining Your Paper	Revising and Editing	- Employ strategies for effective revision - Avoid common pitfalls	[ ] [ ]
	Peer Review Process	- Understand the importance of peer review - Respond constructively to reviewer comments	[ ] [ ]
	Proofreading	- Check for grammar and syntax errors - Ensure consistency and clarity	[ ] [ ]
Chapter 6: Publishing Your Paper	Choosing the Right Journal	- Consider journal scope and audience - Evaluate impact factor and reputation - Understand the peer review process and timeline - Consider publication costs	[ ] [ ] [ ] [ ]
Chapter 7: Submitting Your Paper to a Journal	Submission Guidelines	- Follow the journal's submission guidelines - Prepare a compelling cover letter	[ ] [ ]
	Handling Revisions and Rejections	- Respond to feedback from editors and reviewers - Make necessary revisions - Learn from feedback for future improvements	[ ] [ ] [ ]
Chapter 8: Beyond Publication	Promoting Your Work	- Network at academic conferences - Use social media and research gateways	[ ] [ ]
	Building a Research Profile	- Maintain an updated CV - Engage in continuous learning and development	[ ] [ ]

COVER LETTER TEMPLATE

Purpose: To provide a comprehensive introduction to your manuscript, offering detailed insights into its significance and relevance to the journal.

Components:

- ***Introduction***
  - Manuscript title
  - Type of article (e.g., original research, review article)
- ***Rationale and Significance***
  - Importance of the research
  - Novelty and relevance to the journal's audience
  - Potential impact on the field
- ***Fit with the Journal***
  - Justification of why the manuscript is suitable for the journal
  - Reference to the journal's scope and specific areas addressed by your research
- ***Summary of Key Findings***
  - Brief overview of the main findings and contributions
- ***Detailed Research Context***
  - Background and context of the research
  - How the research fills existing gaps in the literature
- ***Ethical and Conflict of Interest Statements***
  - Statements on ethical approval
  - Disclosure of any conflicts of interest
- ***Contact Information***
  - Author's contact details
  - Willingness to provide additional information if needed

COVER LETTER TEMPLATE EXAMPLE

Section	Content
Introduction	Dear [Editor's Name], I am pleased to submit our manuscript titled "[Manuscript Title]" for your consideration as an [article type] in [Journal Name].
Rationale and Significance	Our research explores [brief description of the research problem]. This study is unique because [highlight the novelty and importance]. It is particularly relevant to the readers of [Journal Name] as it [explain relevance].
Fit with the Journal	We believe our manuscript is a strong fit for [Journal Name] due to [justify suitability]. Our work addresses [specific areas of the journal's focus].
Summary of Key Findings	The main findings of our study are [brief summary of key findings]. These contributions are important because [explain contributions].
Detailed Research Context	The background for our research is [provide context]. Our study aims to fill existing gaps in the literature by [explain how the research addresses gaps].
Ethical and Conflict of Interest Statements	This research was approved by [Ethical Committee], and all participants provided informed consent. We have no conflicts of interest to disclose.
Contact Information	Thank you for considering our manuscript. Please feel free to contact me at [email] or [phone number] if you need any further information. Sincerely, [Your Name]

RESPONSE TO REVIEWERS TEMPLATE

Purpose: To provide a structured format for responding to reviewers' comments after the peer review process.

Components:

- ***Thank You Note***
  - Express gratitude to the reviewers for their valuable feedback.
- ***Response to Comments***
  - List each reviewer's comment followed by your response.
  - Clearly indicate any changes made to the manuscript in response to the comments.
  - Provide a rationale for any suggestions that were not adopted.
- ***Summary of Changes***
  - Briefly summarize the major changes made to the manuscript in response to the reviewers' comments.

Example

Section	Content
Thank You Note	We sincerely thank the reviewers for their valuable feedback and suggestions. We have carefully considered each comment and made the necessary revisions to improve our manuscript. Below are our detailed responses to each comment.
Response to Reviewer 1	**Comment 1:** [Reviewer's comment] **Response:** [Your response, detailing changes made] **Changes:** [Specific changes in the manuscript]
	Comment 2: [Reviewer's comment] **Response:** [Your response, detailing changes made] **Changes:** [Specific changes in the manuscript]
Response to Reviewer 2	**Comment 1:** [Reviewer's comment] **Response:** [Your response, detailing changes made] **Changes:** [Specific changes in the manuscript]
	Comment 2: [Reviewer's comment] **Response:** [Your response, detailing changes made] **Changes:** [Specific changes in the manuscript]
Summary of Changes	The major changes made to the manuscript include [brief summary of major changes].

TARGET JOURNAL EVALUATION TEMPLATE FOR SUBMISSION

Criteria	Details	Rating
Journal Name:		
Journal Website:		
1. Scope and Audience		
Research Scope:	Does the journal's scope align with your research topic?	[Yes/No]
	Specific areas of focus that match your research:	
Target Audience:	Who is the primary audience of this journal? (e.g., researchers, practitioners, policymakers)	
	Relevance to your research community:	[High/Medium/Low]
2. Journal Quality and Impact		
Impact Factor:	Latest impact factor:	
	5-year impact factor (if available):	
Reputation:	Reputation within your field:	[High/Medium/Low]
	Ranking in relevant academic databases (e.g., SCImago, Google Scholar Metrics):	
Indexing:	Indexed in major databases (e.g., PubMed, Web of Science, Scopus):	[Yes/No]
	Other indexing services:	
3. Submission Guidelines		
Manuscript Requirements:	Word limit:	
	Required sections (e.g., abstract, keywords, introduction, methods, results, discussion, references)	
	Specific formatting guidelines (font, margins, line spacing):	
Submission Process:	Online submission system:	[Yes/No]

	Typical time from submission to first decision:	
Types of Articles Accepted:	Original research:	[Yes/No]
	Review articles:	[Yes/No]
	Case studies:	[Yes/No]
	Short communications:	[Yes/No]
	Other types:	
4. Publication Fees		
Article Processing Charges (APCs):	Amount: $	
	Open access options:	[Yes/No]
	Waivers or discounts available:	[Yes/No]
Submission Fees:	Amount (if any): $	
Additional Charges:	Page charges:	[Yes/No]
	Color figure charges:	[Yes/No]
	Supplementary material fees:	[Yes/No]
5. Review Process		
Peer Review Type:	Double-blind peer review:	[Yes/No]
	Single-blind peer review:	[Yes/No]
	Open peer review:	[Yes/No]
Average Review Time:	From submission to first decision:	
	Total time to publication:	
Review Process Transparency:	Clear description of the review process on the journal website:	[Yes/No]
6. Ethical Considerations		
Ethical Standards:	Adherence to ethical guidelines (e.g., COPE):	[Yes/No]
	Policies on plagiarism, data fabrication, and conflicts of interest:	[Yes/No]
Author Rights:	Authors retain copyright:	[Yes/No]
	Policy on sharing and reuse of published work:	
7. Additional Factors		
Editorial Board:	Notable editors and their affiliations:	
	Diversity and expertise of the editorial board:	[High/Medium/Low]
Engagement and Interaction:	Active on social media:	[Yes/No]

	Opportunities for reader engagement (e.g., forums, webinars):	[Yes/No]
Open Access and Reach:	Open access options:	[Yes/No]
	Global vs. regional audience reach:	

8. Overall Evaluation

Strengths:	List key strengths of the journal.	
Weaknesses:	List key weaknesses or concerns.	
Recommendation:	Based on your evaluation, is this journal a good fit for your research?	[Yes/No]

PUBLICATION TIMELINE TEMPLATE

Purpose: The publication timeline template helps map out the entire process from manuscript preparation to submission, ensuring every step is completed on schedule.

Task	**Start Date**	**End Date**	Notes
Manuscript Preparation			
Drafting First Manuscript			Complete initial draft
Internal Review			Collect feedback from co-authors
Final Edits			Incorporate feedback and finalize
Data Collection and Analysis			
Data Collection Start			Begin collecting data
Data Collection End			Complete data collection
Data Analysis			Analyze and interpret data
Literature Review			
Initial Literature Review			Conduct thorough literature review
Ongoing Updates to Literature Review			Periodic updates as new studies are published
Writing Sections			
Writing Introduction			Draft and finalize introduction
Writing Methods			Draft and finalize methods section
Writing Results			Draft and finalize results section
Writing Discussion			Draft and finalize discussion
Submission Preparation			
Writing Cover Letter			Write and revise cover letter
Formatting Manuscript			Format according to guidelines
Preparing References			Ensure all references are correct and formatted
Submission			
Submission Deadline			Set target submission date
Submission Checklist Review			Ensure all requirements are met
Post-Submission			
Follow-Up on Submission			Check status and respond to requests promptly

SOFTWARE AND ONLINE TOOLS

In the journey of academic writing, managing references and ensuring the originality of your work are crucial elements that require careful attention. To aid in this process, various tools have been developed to help researchers maintain accuracy, organization, and integrity in their writing.

Reference management tools like EndNote, Zotero, and Mendeley are indispensable for organizing citations, creating bibliographies, and ensuring consistency in your references.

Similarly, plagiarism checkers such as Turnitin and Grammarly play a vital role in safeguarding the originality of your work by detecting potential issues before submission. In this section, comprehensive checklists are presented to guide you in effectively incorporating these tools into your writing process, streamlining your workflow, and upholding the highest standards of academic integrity.

REFERENCE MANAGEMENT TOOLS

Category	Details
Introduction to Reference Managers	
Overview of Reference Managers	Reference managers like EndNote, Zotero, and Mendeley are software tools designed to help researchers organize and manage their references and citations.
Why Use a Reference Manager?	These tools streamline the process of collecting, organizing, citing, and sharing references, saving time and reducing the risk of citation errors.
Comparison of Popular Tools	**EndNote**: A powerful tool with advanced features, suitable for researchers with extensive bibliographic needs.
	Zotero: An open-source, user-friendly option, ideal for collaborative work and integration with web browsers.
	Mendeley: Combines reference management with a social network, allowing researchers to connect and collaborate while managing their references.
How to Use These Tools Effectively	
Setting Up the Tool	**Installation**: Download and install your chosen reference manager (EndNote, Zotero, or Mendeley) from the official website.
	Creating an Account: Sign up for an account to enable cloud storage and syncing across devices (important for Zotero and Mendeley).
Importing References	**Manual Entry**: Learn to manually input references by filling out fields such as author, title, publication year, journal, etc.
	Automatic Import: Use browser extensions or import options to automatically capture references from databases, websites, or PDFs.
Organizing Your Library	**Folders and Tags**: Create folders or collections to organize references by project, subject, or theme. Use tags for additional categorization.
	Notes and Annotations: Add notes to individual references for quick recall of important details or ideas. Annotate PDFs directly within the tool.
Citation Management	**In-Text Citations**: Integrate your reference manager with word processors (e.g., MS Word, Google Docs) to insert in-text citations as you write.
	Citation Styles: Select the appropriate citation style (e.g., APA, MLA, Chicago) from the tool's library of styles to ensure consistency.

	Generating Bibliographies: Automatically generate and format your bibliography based on the citations used in your document.
Collaborative Features	**Sharing Libraries**: Share your reference library with collaborators or export references for others to use.
	Group Work: Use group libraries (available in Zotero and Mendeley) to collaborate on reference management in team projects.
Backing Up and Syncing	**Cloud Syncing**: Enable syncing across multiple devices to keep your reference library up-to-date wherever you are.
	Backup Options: Regularly back up your reference library to avoid data loss. Tools often provide options for local and cloud backups.
Advanced Features	**Advanced Search**: Utilize advanced search functions to quickly locate references using keywords, tags, or other criteria.
	Custom Citation Styles: Learn to create or modify citation styles if the standard options don't meet your specific needs.
	Importing from Other Tools: If switching from another reference manager, import your existing library into your new tool.
Troubleshooting and Support	**Common Issues**: Familiarize yourself with common issues (e.g., citation errors, syncing problems) and how to resolve them.
	Support Resources: Use available resources such as user guides, forums, and customer support for troubleshooting and learning new features.

COMPREHENSIVE TABLE FOR PLAGIARISM CHECKERS

Category	Details
Introduction to Plagiarism Checkers	
Overview of Plagiarism Checkers	Plagiarism checkers like Turnitin and Grammarly are essential tools designed to ensure the originality of your work by detecting similarities with existing content.
Why Use a Plagiarism Checker?	These tools help identify unintentional plagiarism, ensuring your work maintains academic integrity and complies with ethical standards.
Comparison of Popular Tools	**Turnitin**: Widely used in academic institutions, Turnitin provides a comprehensive similarity report, highlighting potential instances of plagiarism.
	Grammarly: While primarily a grammar checker, Grammarly includes a built-in plagiarism detection feature, making it a versatile tool for writers.
How to Use These Tools Effectively	
Setting Up the Tool	**Creating an Account**: Sign up for a Turnitin or Grammarly account, either through your institution or independently, to access plagiarism detection features.
Submitting Your Document	**File Upload**: Upload your document to the plagiarism checker. Turnitin typically requires institutional access, while Grammarly offers individual options.
Understanding the Similarity Report	**Similarity Score**: Review the similarity percentage provided by the tool, indicating how much of your content matches existing sources.
	Detailed Report: Examine the detailed report that highlights specific sections of text that match other sources. This helps identify where citation or rephrasing is needed.
Addressing Potential Plagiarism	**Rewriting**: For flagged sections, consider rewriting the text in your own words to enhance originality.
	Proper Citation: Ensure that all properly cited content is correctly formatted according to the required citation style to avoid false positives.
Integration with Writing Process	**Use During Drafting**: Utilize plagiarism checkers at multiple stages of writing to catch issues early and refine your work.
	Final Check: Perform a final plagiarism check before submission to ensure all content is original and properly cited.
Additional Features	**Grammar and Style Checking**: Tools like Grammarly offer grammar and style suggestions alongside

	plagiarism detection, providing a more polished final document.
	Institutional Access: Turnitin is often integrated with learning management systems (LMS) like Blackboard or Moodle, allowing direct submission from these platforms.
Troubleshooting and Support	**False Positives**: Be aware that plagiarism checkers may flag common phrases or properly cited references as plagiarism—review these cases carefully.
	Support Resources: Use available support resources, such as help centers and tutorials, to better understand how to interpret reports and resolve issues.

COMPREHENSIVE PLAGIARISM CHECKLIST FOR SCIENTIFIC PAPERS

Category	Task	Checked
Understanding Plagiarism		
Definition of Plagiarism	Ensure you fully understand what constitutes plagiarism, including direct copying, paraphrasing without attribution, and self-plagiarism.	[ ]
Types of Plagiarism	Familiarize yourself with the different types of plagiarism: verbatim plagiarism, mosaic plagiarism, and accidental plagiarism.	[ ]
Originality of Content		
Original Writing	Ensure all writing is original and in your own words, except for properly cited quotes.	[ ]
Paraphrasing Techniques	Learn effective paraphrasing techniques to rephrase ideas while retaining the original meaning.	[ ]
Proper Attribution	Always give proper credit to the original source when using ideas, data, or text that are not your own.	[ ]
Citation and Referencing		
Accurate Citations	Ensure all sources are accurately cited according to the journal's required citation style (e.g., APA, MLA, Chicago).	[ ]
Consistent Referencing	Maintain consistency in citation format throughout the paper, including in-text citations and the reference list.	[ ]
Quotation Marks	Use quotation marks for direct quotes and cite the source immediately following the quote.	[ ]
Use of Plagiarism Checkers		
Run Plagiarism Check	Use a plagiarism detection tool (e.g., Turnitin, Grammarly) to check for unintentional plagiarism before submission.	[ ]
Analyze Similarity Report	Review the similarity report to identify any sections that may need rewriting or additional citations.	[ ]
Address Flagged Content	Rewrite or properly cite any content that has been flagged by the plagiarism checker to ensure originality.	[ ]

Handling Common Issues		
Common Knowledge	Understand that common knowledge does not require citation, but be cautious with borderline cases.	[ ]
Proper Citation of Figures	Ensure all figures, tables, and images used from other sources are properly cited and permission is obtained if necessary.	[ ]
Self-Plagiarism	Avoid reusing your previously published work without proper citation or permission, as this constitutes self-plagiarism.	[ ]
Final Verification		
Double-Check All Citations	Review all in-text citations and references to ensure they are complete and correctly formatted.	[ ]
Final Plagiarism Check	Perform a final plagiarism check after making all revisions to ensure no new issues have been introduced.	[ ]
Compliance with Guidelines	Ensure your paper complies with the ethical guidelines on plagiarism as set by your institution or journal.	[ ]
Ethical Considerations		
Proper Acknowledgment	Ensure all contributors and sources are properly acknowledged, including in the acknowledgments section of your paper.	[ ]
Ethical Use of AI Tools	If AI tools (e.g., ChatGPT) were used, ensure that their contributions are properly acknowledged and that the work remains original.	[ ]
Institutional Guidelines	Review and adhere to any specific plagiarism policies or guidelines provided by your institution or funding body.	[ ]

ONE LAST THING

If you found this book useful and enjoyed reading it, I would be grateful if you would post a review. Your support really makes a difference. I read all the reviews personally so I can receive your suggestions and make this book even better.

Thank you for your support!

MORE FROM THE MASTERING RESEARCH SERIES

REFERENCES

1.   Willis LD. Formulating the Research Question and Framing the Hypothesis. Respir Care. 2023 Aug;68(8):1180–5.

2.   Zevia SchneiderDean Dean Whitehead. Identifying research ideas, questions, statements and hypotheses. In: Nursing and Midwifery Research: Methods and Appraisal for Evidence Based Practice.

3.   Barroga E, Matanguihan GJ. A Practical Guide to Writing Quantitative and Qualitative Research Questions and Hypotheses in Scholarly Articles. J Korean Med Sci. 2022;37(16).

4.   Clarivate. Journal Citation Reports [Internet]. 2024 [cited 2024 Dec 5]. Available from: https://clarivate.com/academia-government/scientific-and-academic-research/research-funding-analytics/journal-citation-reports/

5.   Scimago. Scimago Journal & Country Rank [Internet]. 2024 [cited 2024 Dec 5]. Available from: https://www.scimagojr.com/

6.   Mohsin Hassan Alvi. A Manual for Referencing Styles in Research [Internet]. 2016 [cited 2024 Dec 5]. Available from: https://www.researchgate.net/profile/Mohsin-Alvi/publication/308786787_A_Manual_for_Referencing_Styles_in_Research/links/57f14ed008ae8da3ce4ec234/A-Manual-for-Referencing-Styles-in-Research.pdf

7.   University of Reading. Styles of referencing [Internet]. 2024 [cited 2024 Dec 5]. Available from: https://libguides.reading.ac.uk/citing-references/referencingstyles

8.   Ogbeiwi O. Why written objectives need to be really SMART. British Journal of Healthcare Management. 2017 Jul 2;23(7):324–36.

9.   Bjerke MB, Renger R. Being smart about writing SMART objectives. Eval Program Plann. 2017 Apr;61:125–7.

10.   Lorenzetti DL, Ghali WA. Reference management software for systematic reviews and meta-analyses: an exploration of usage and usability. BMC Med Res Methodol. 2013 Dec 15;13(1):141.

11. COPE. Committee on Publication Ethics [Internet]. 2024 [cited 2024 Dec 5]. Available from: https://publicationethics.org/

12. Tharib S. Blurring the Boundaries: Exploring the Classification of Artificial Life in Robotics and AI. 2024.

13. Page MJ, McKenzie JE, Bossuyt PM, Boutron I, Hoffmann TC, Mulrow CD, et al. The PRISMA 2020 statement: an updated guideline for reporting systematic reviews. BMJ [Internet]. 2021 Mar 29;n71. Available from: https://www.bmj.com/lookup/doi/10.1136/bmj.n71

www.ingramcontent.com/pod-product-compliance
Lightning Source LLC
LaVergne TN
LVHW060557200726
843509LV00003B/140